Learn Numbers
with Camron and Chloe

Denver International SchoolHouse

Learn Numbers with Camron and Chloe

Denver International SchoolHouse

© 2021 Denver International SchoolHouse

All rights reserved. No part of this publication may be reproduced, stored in a retrieval system or transmited in any form or by any means, electronic, mechanical, photocopying, recording or otherwise without the prior permision of the publisher or in accordance with the provisions of the Copyright, Designs and Patents Act 1988 or under the terms of any licence permitting limited copying issued by the Copyright Licensing Angency.

ISBN : 9978-1-7358013-8-4

Name:_____

One

Color the number 1. Color the strawberry.

Trace the number 1.

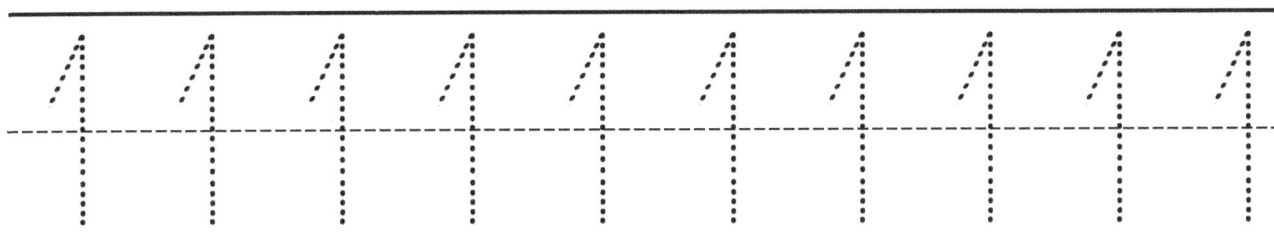

Circle the box showing 1.

 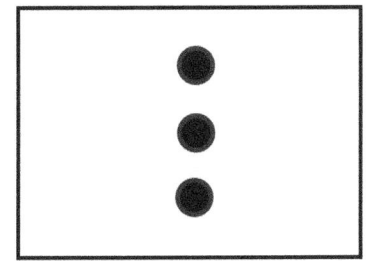 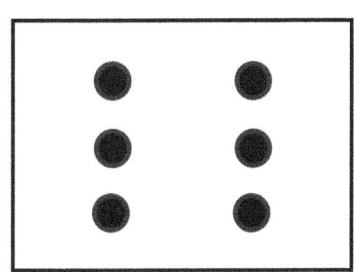

Denver International SchoolHouse

Name:_____

One

Color only the number 1.

3	1	5
4	6	1
2	6	1	3	5
1	4	2	5	6
6	2	1
4	1	3

1

Denver International SchoolHouse

Name:_____

Color

Write

Search and color

3

Denver International SchoolHouse

Name:_____

One

Trace.

Use stickers to show the number.

Find the number 1

| 6 | 1 | 4 | 2 | 3 | 5 |
| 1 | 4 | 3 | 1 | 2 | 6 |

Subtract one and add one.

  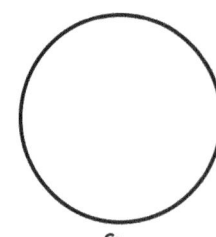

before   after

Color the feathers according to the number.

Practice writing.   One

Denver International SchoolHouse

Name:_____

One

Trace the number. Trace the number word.

1　1　1　1　1　1

One　One

One　One

Now, practice writing the number and the number word on your own.

5　　Denver International SchoolHouse

Name:_____

One

Color one rocket.

Denver International SchoolHouse

Name:_____

Two

Color the number 2. Color the 2 ducks.

Trace the number 2.

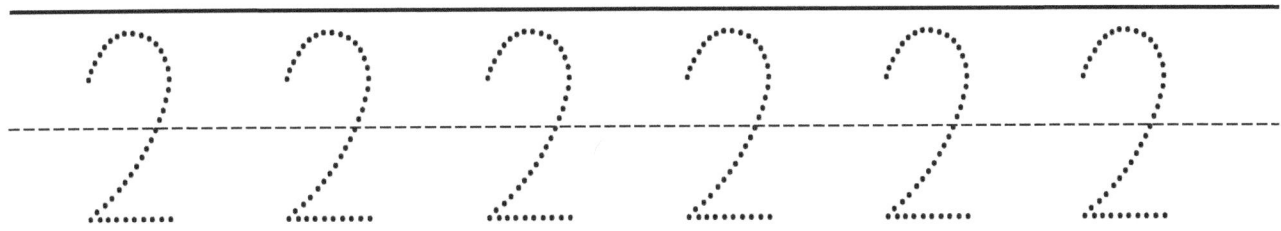

Circle the box showing 2.

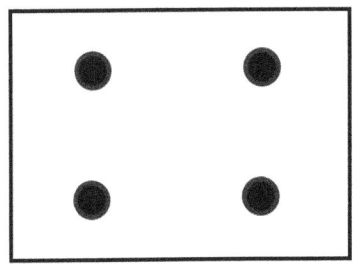 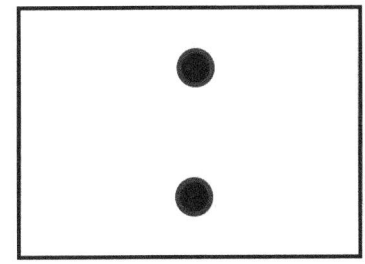 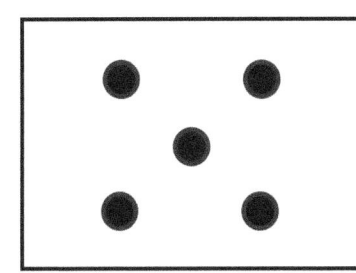

Name:_____

Two

Color only the number 2.

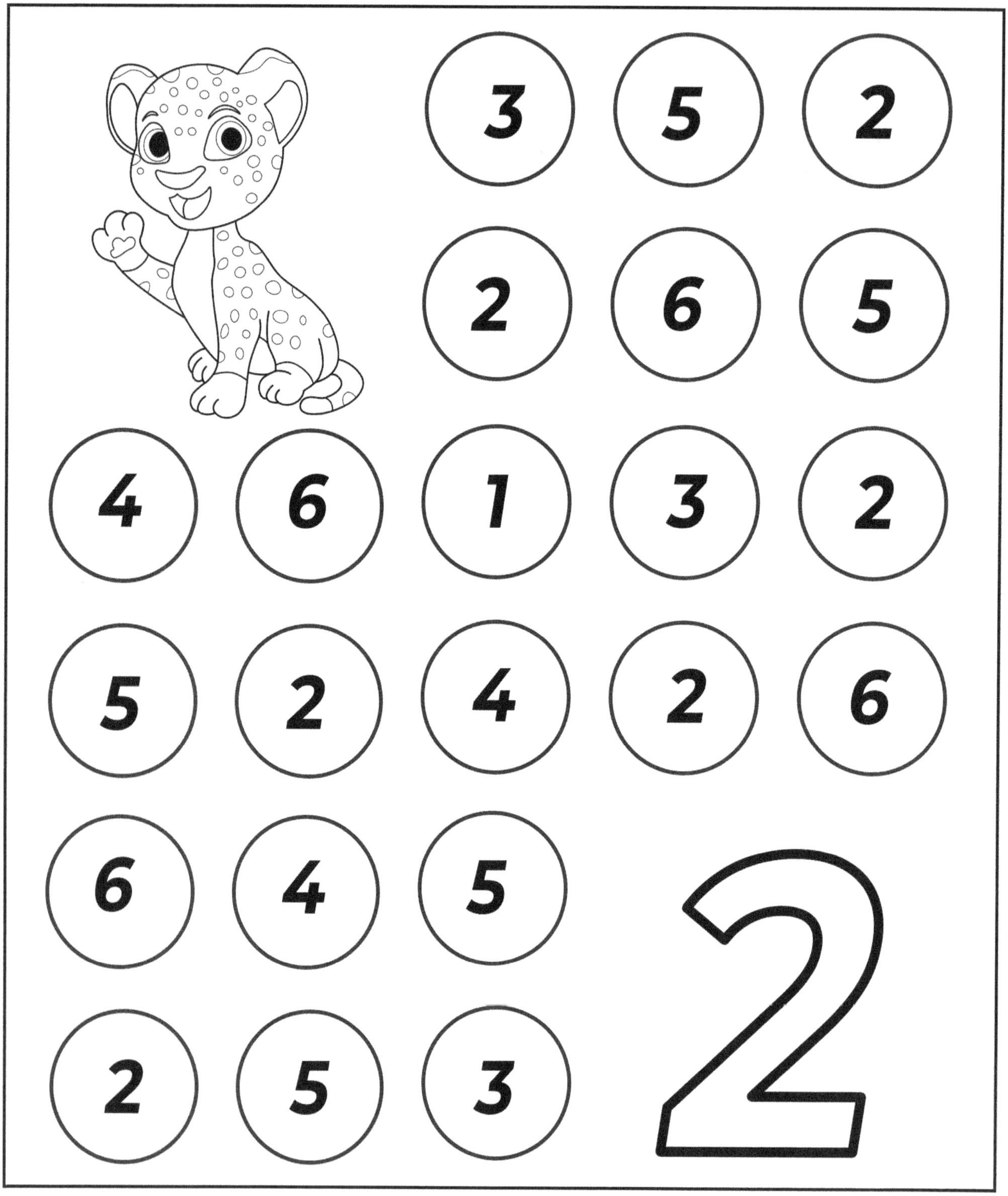

3	5	2
2	6	5
4	6	1	3	2
5	2	4	2	6
6	4	5
2	5	3

2

Name: _____

Color

Write

Search and color

Name:_____

Two

Trace.

Use stickers to show the number.

Find the number 2.

Subtract one and add one.

  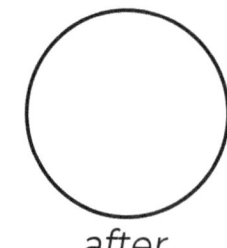

before   after

```
2 6 5 2 3 1
4 1 2 5 2 3
```

Color the feathers according to the number.

Practice writing.   Two

Denver International SchoolHouse   10

Name:_____

Two

Trace the number. Trace the number word.

2 2 2 2 2

Two Two

Two Two

Now, practice writing the number and the number word on your own.

Name:_____

Two

Color two dolphins.

Name:_____

Three

Color the number 3. Color the 3 geese.

Trace the number 3.

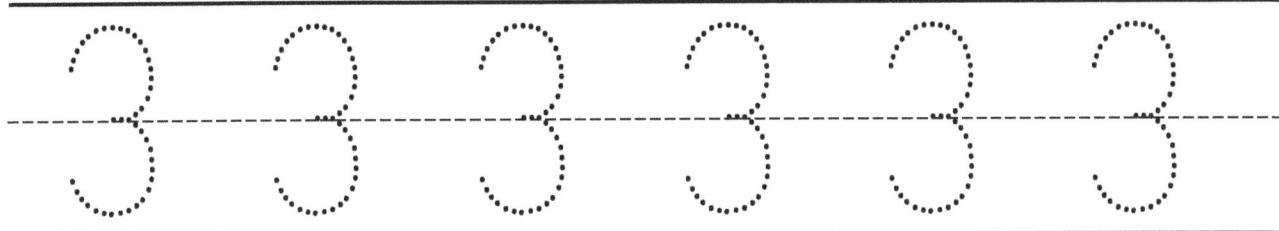

Circle the box showing 3.

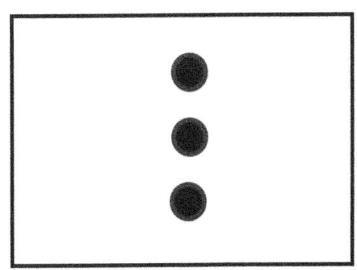 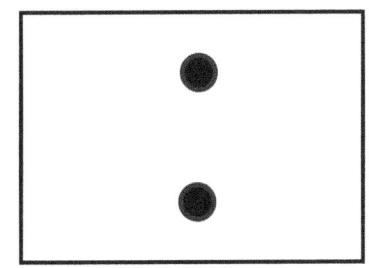 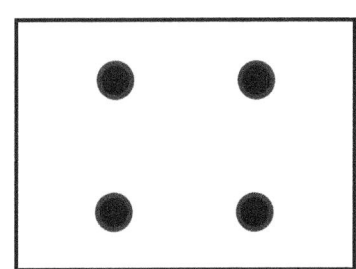

Name:_____

Three

Color only the number 3.

	2	5	3
	6	3	1
3	5	1	2	3
1	3	5	4	6
3	4	5		
1	2	3		

Denver International SchoolHouse

Name: _____

Color

Write

Search and color

Name:_____

Three

Trace.

Use stickers to show the number.

Find the number 3.

3 5 1 2 3 4
1 5 3 3 2 5

Subtract one and add one.

  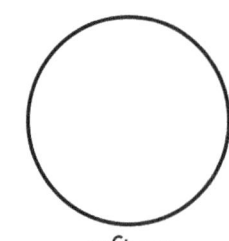

before   after

Color the feathers according to the number.

Practice writing.   Three

Denver International SchoolHouse   16

Name:_____

Three

Trace the number. Trace the number word.

3 3 3 3 3

Three Three

Three Three

Now, practice writing the number and the number word on your own.

Denver International SchoolHouse

Name:_____

Three

Color three cars.

Name:_____

Four

Color the number 4. Color the 4 sunflowers.

Trace the number 4.

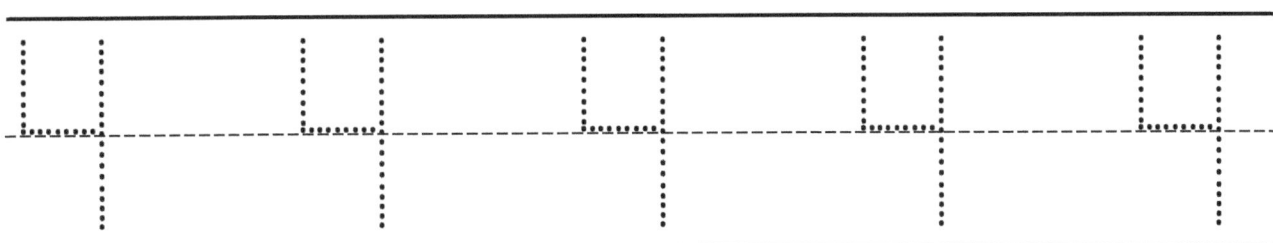

Circle the box showing 4.

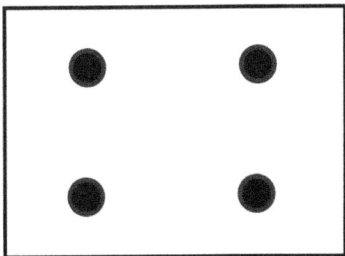 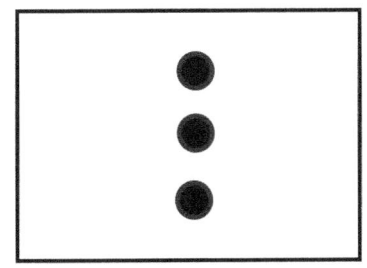 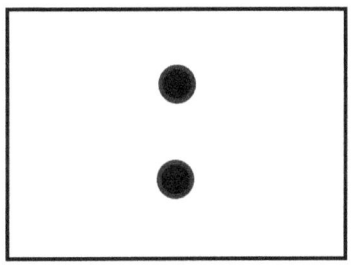

Denver International SchoolHouse

Name:_____

Four

Color only the number 4.

1	5	4
2	4	5
4	7	1	3	2
5	8	4	2	6
1	4	5
4	5	3

Denver International SchoolHouse

Name: _____

Color

Write

Search and color 🖍

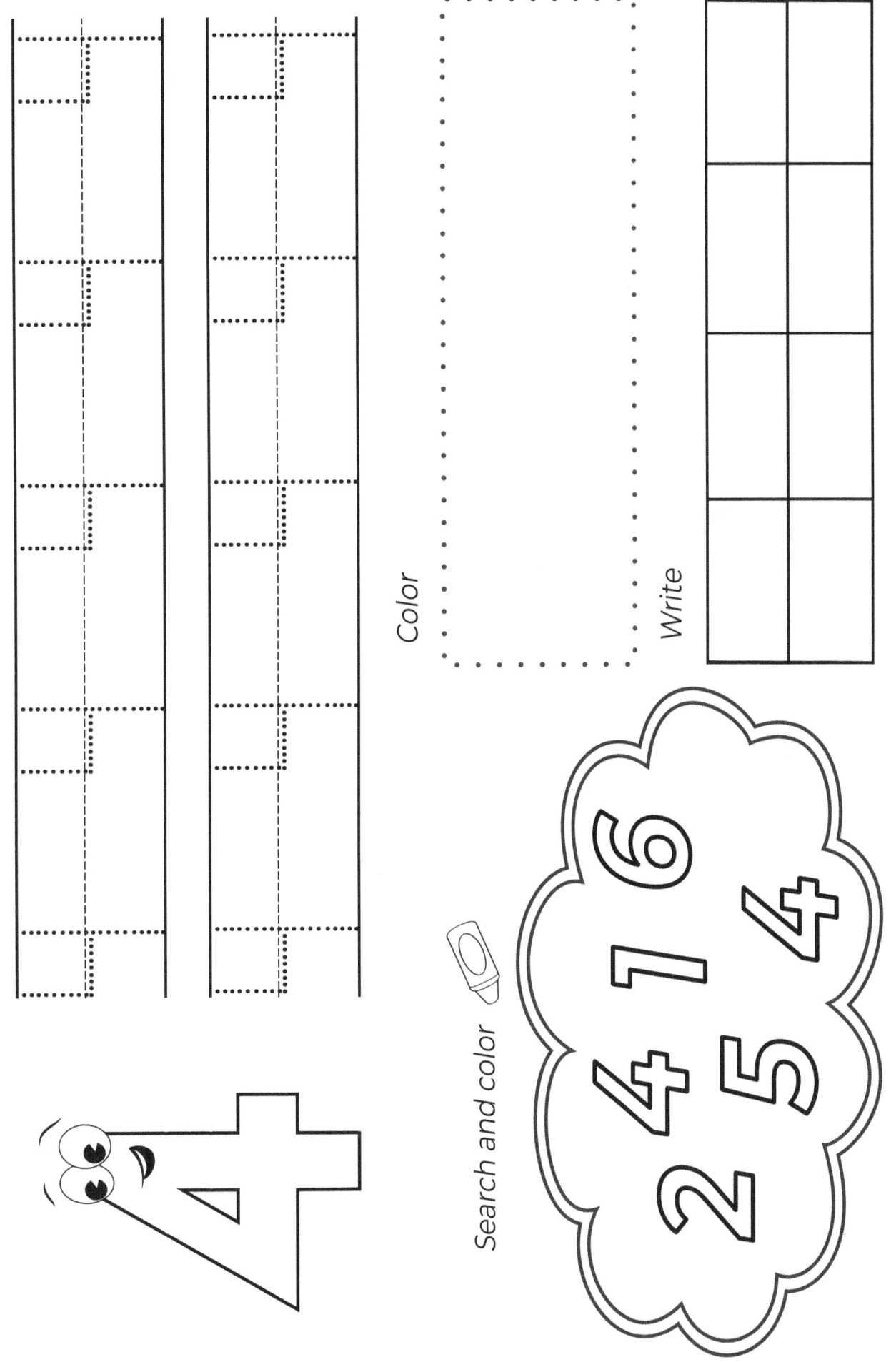

Name:_____

Four

Trace.

Use stickers to show the number.

Find the number 4.

Subtract one and add one.

3 4 5 6 4 1
4 5 3 2 1 6

before

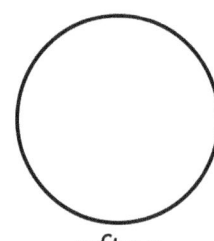
after

Color the feathers according to the number.

Practice writing.   four

Denver International SchoolHouse   22

Name:_____

Four

Trace the number. Trace the number word.

4 4 4 4 4

Four Four

Four Four

Now, practice writing the number and the number word on your own.

Name:_____

Four

Color four pencils.

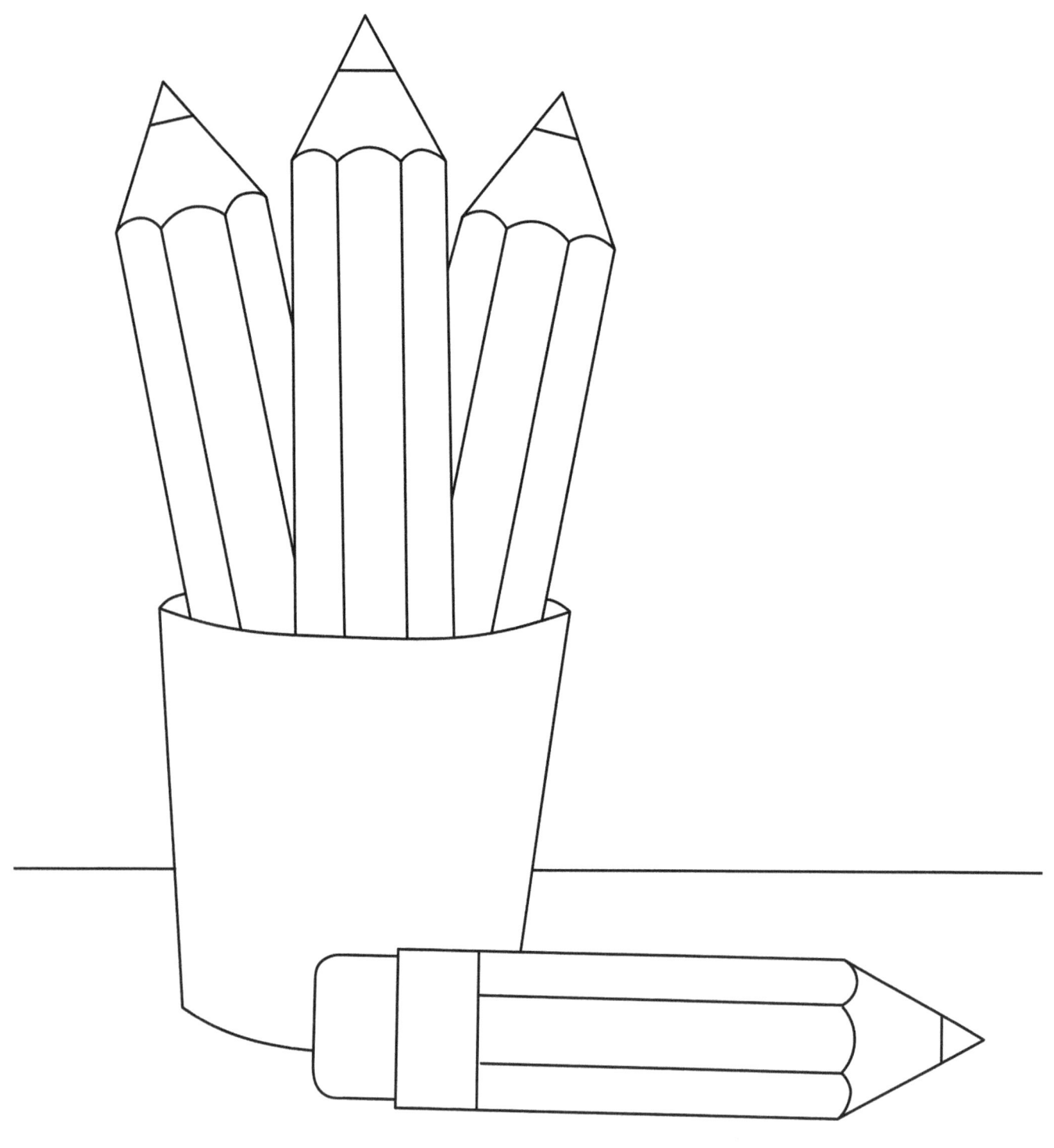

Denver International SchoolHouse

Name:_____

Five

Color the number 5. Color the 5 sheep.

Trace the number 5.

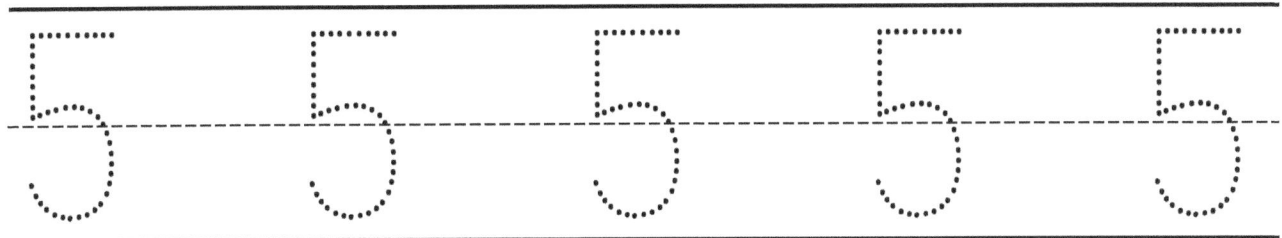

Circle the box showing 5.

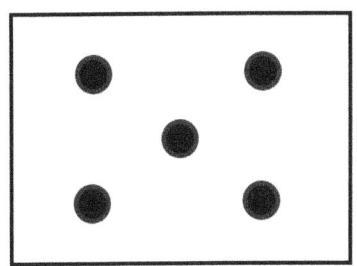 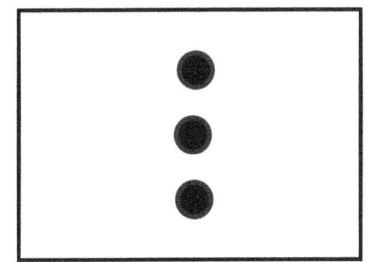 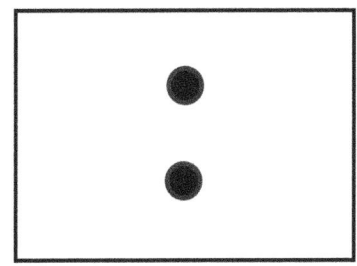

Name:_____

Five

Color only the number 5.

6	5	4
2	3	5
6	7	5	3	2
5	3	4	2	6
7	4	5
4	5	8

5

Denver International SchoolHouse

Name:_____

Color

Write

Search and color

27   Denver International SchoolHouse

Name:_____

Five

Trace.

Use stickers to show the number.

Find the number 5.

Subtract one and add one.

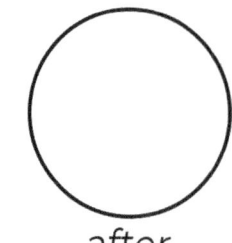

before   after

Color the feathers according to the number.

Practice writing.   Five

Denver International SchoolHouse   28

Name:_____

Five

Trace the number. Trace the number word.

5 5 5 5 5

Five Five

Five Five

Now, practice writing the number and the number word on your own.

Name:_____

Five

Color five cats.

Denver International SchoolHouse

Name:_____

Six

Color the number 6. Color the 6 clouds.

Trace the number 6.

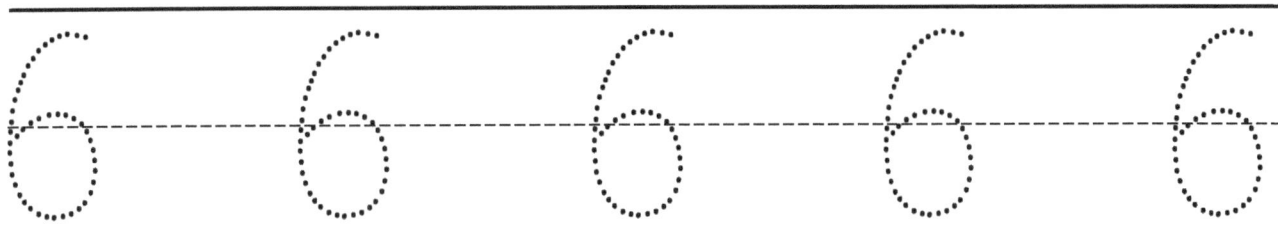

Circle the box showing 6.

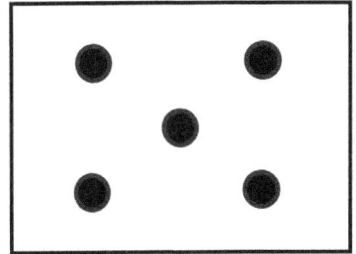 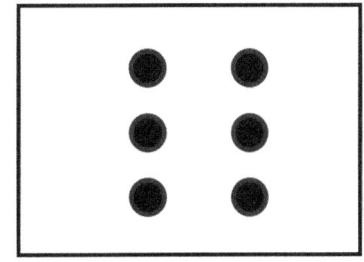 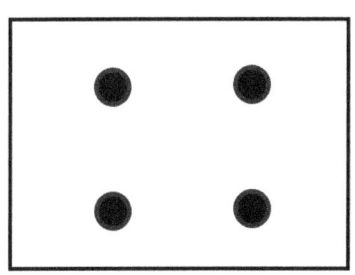

Denver International SchoolHouse

Name:_____

Six

Color only the number 6.

6	3	2
2	6	5
6	8	5	9	2
1	3	6	2	6
6	9	5
4	6	8

6

Denver International SchoolHouse

Name: _____

Color

Write

Search and color

Name:_____

Six

Trace

Use stickers to show the number.

Find the number 6.

Subtract one and add one.

6 4 5 6 1 3
9 6 8 6 7 5

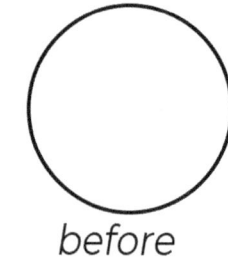
before

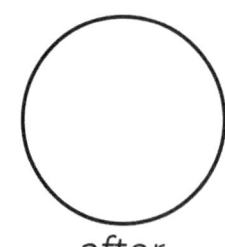
after

Color the feathers according to the number.

Practice writing. Six   Six

Denver International SchoolHouse   34

Name:_____

Six

Trace the number. Trace the number word.

6 6 6 6 6

Six Six

Six Six

Now, practice writing the number and the number word on your own.

Name:_____

Six

Color six balls.

Name:_____

Seven

Color the number 7. Color the 7 balls.

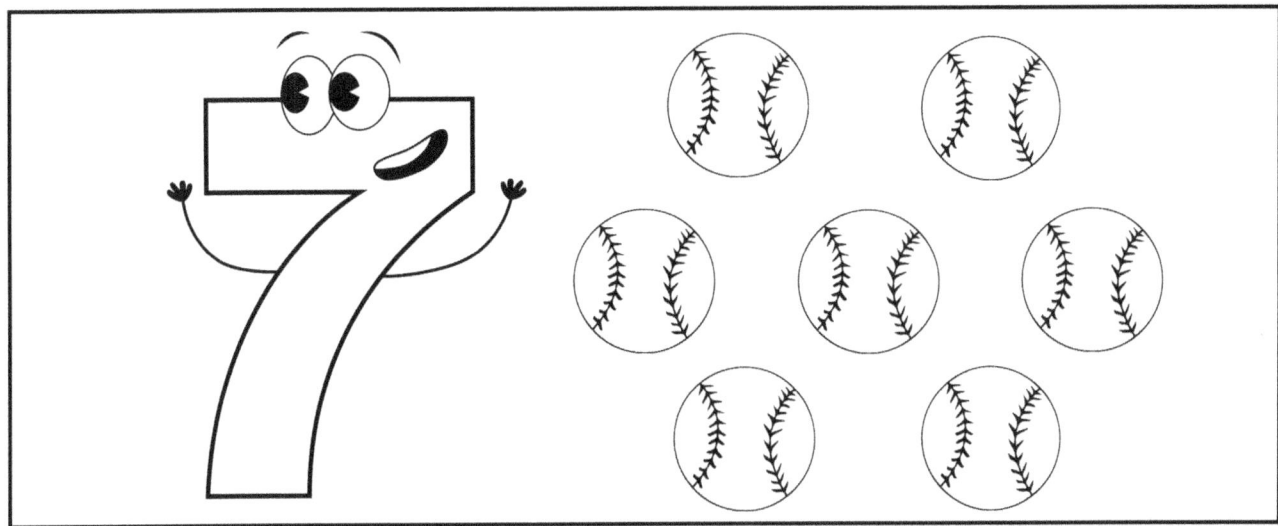

Trace the number 7.

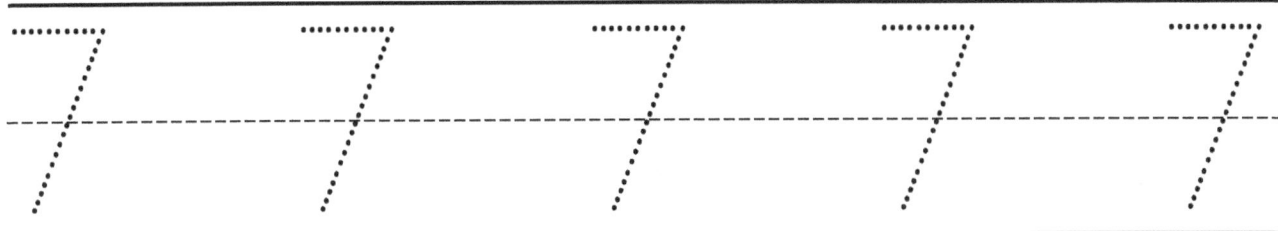

Circle the box showing 7.

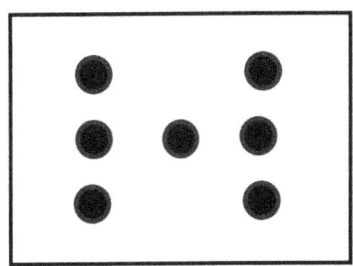 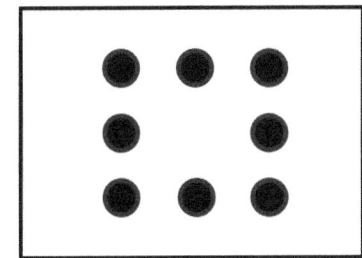 

37   Denver International SchoolHouse

Name:_____

Seven

Color only the number 7.

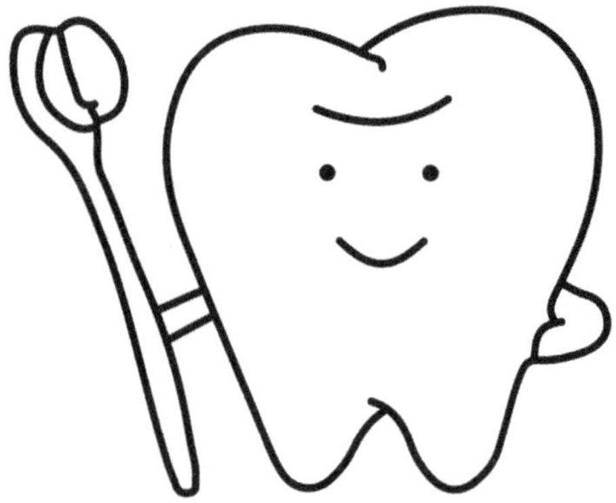

| 7 | 5 | 4 |
| 2 | 7 | 9 |

3 7 5 8 1

9 3 7 2 7

7 4 5

3 7 8

7

Denver International SchoolHouse

Name:_____

Color

Write

Search and color

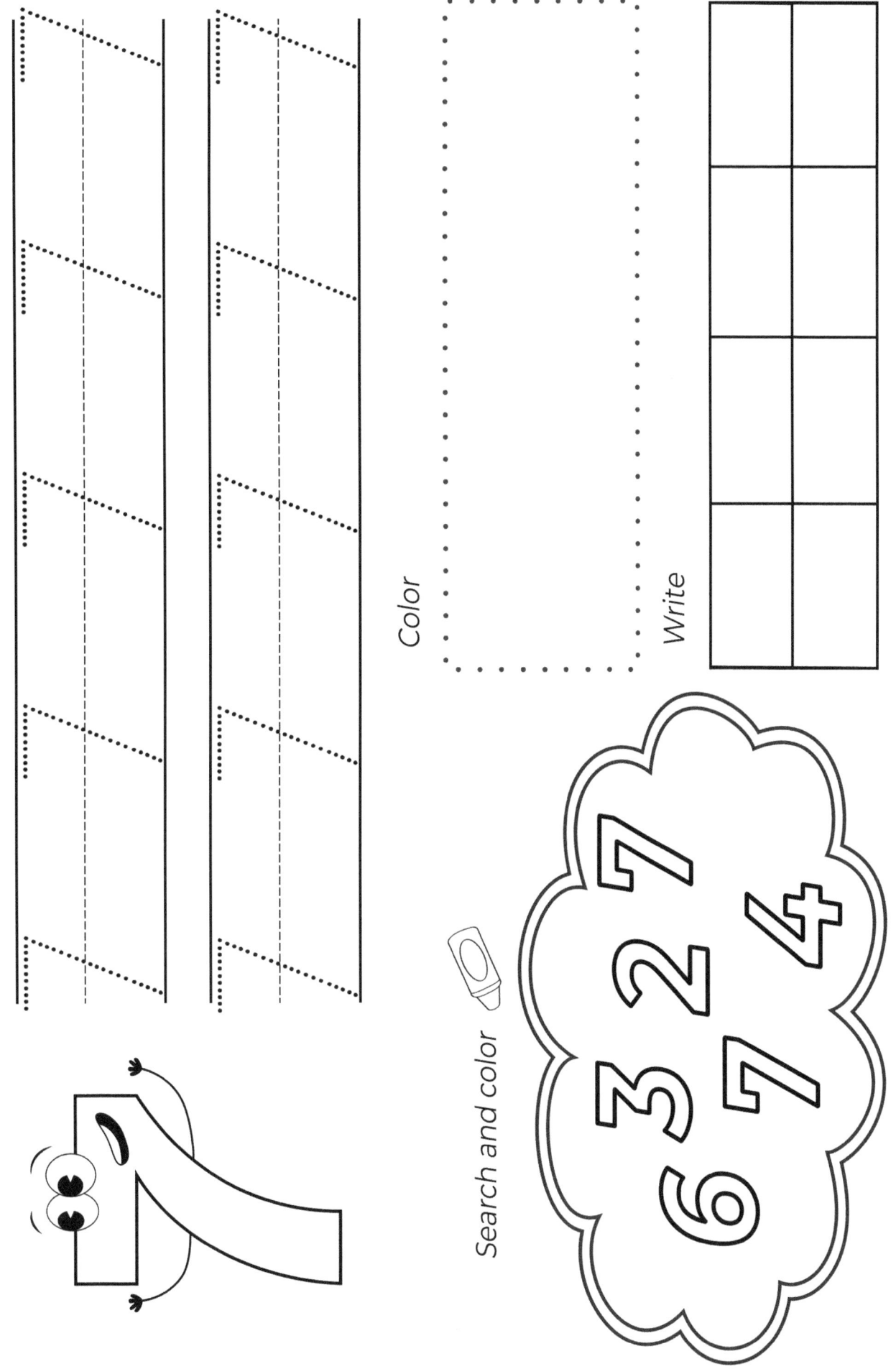

Name:_____

Seven

Trace.

Use stickers to show the number.

Find the number 7.

Subtract one and add one.

7 8 9 7 6 5
9 8 7 6 5 4

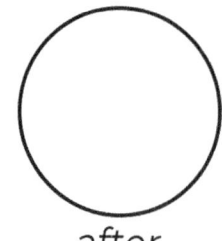

before   after

Color the feathers according to the number.

Practice writing.   Seven

Denver International SchoolHouse   40

Name:_____

Seven

Trace the number. Trace the number word.

7 7 7 7 7

Seven Seven

Seven Seven

Now, practice writing the number and the number word on your own.

Denver International SchoolHouse

Name:_____

Seven

Color seven kites.

Denver International SchoolHouse 42

Name:_____

Eight

Color the number 8. Color the 8 balls.

Trace the number 8.

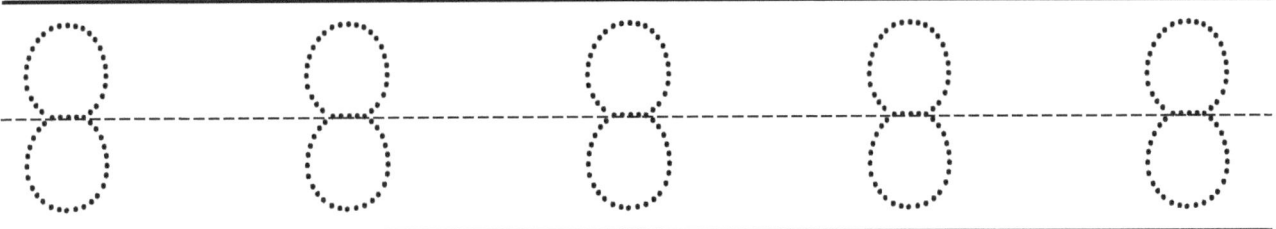

Circle the box showing 8.

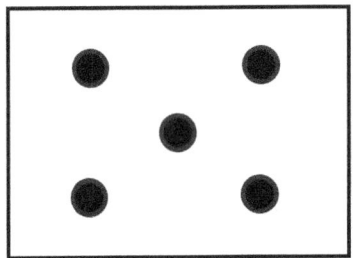 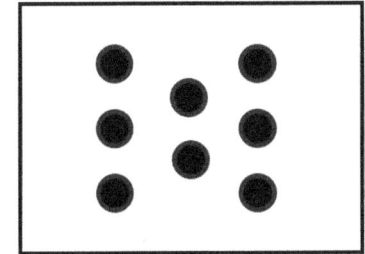 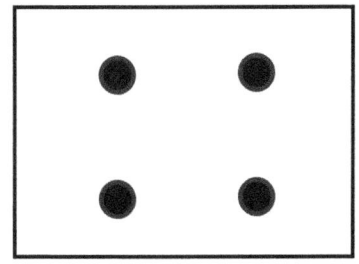

Name:_____

Eight

Color only the number 8.

8	3	9
2	8	10

11	8	10	9	2
8	7	6	8	6

6	9	8
10	6	8

8

Denver International SchoolHouse

Name: _____

Color

Write

Search and color

Name:_____

Eight

Trace.

Use stickers to show the number.

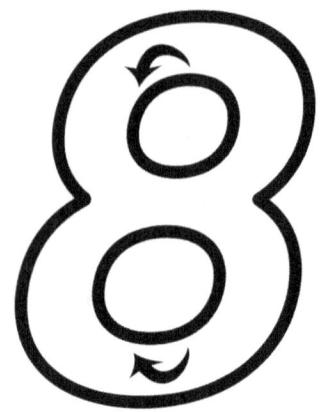

Find the number 8.

Subtract one and add one.

```
9 8 7 6 5 8
5 6 8 7 3 1
```

before

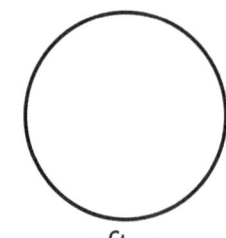
after

Color the feathers according to the number.

Practice writing.   Eight

Denver International SchoolHouse

Name:_____

Eight

Trace the number. Trace the number word.

8 8 8 8 8

Eight Eight

Eight Eight

Now, practice writing the number and the number word on your own.

_____

- -

_____

- -

_____

Denver International SchoolHouse

Eight

Color eight fish.

Name:_____

Nine

Color the number 9. Color the 9 apples.

Trace the number 9.

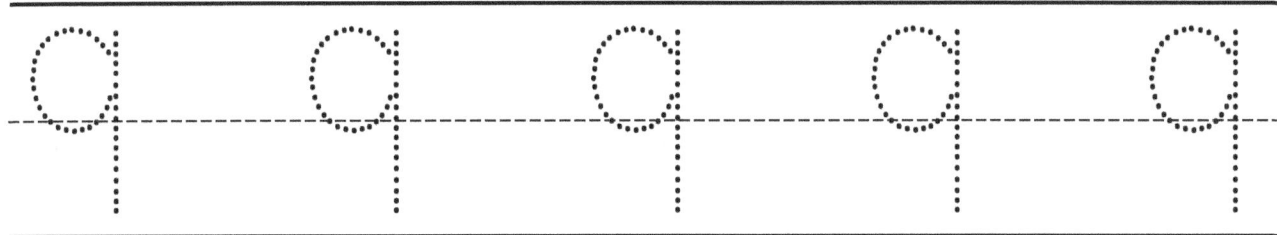

Circle the box showing 9.

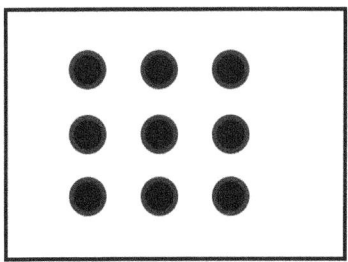 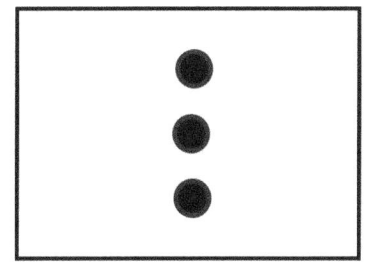 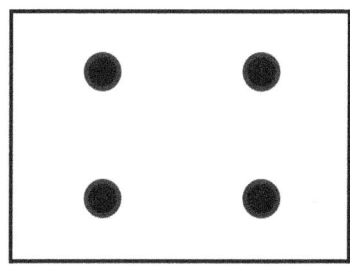

Name:_____

Nine

Color only the number 9.

6	9	11
2	10	9
8	9	5	9	2
5	11	4	12	9
7	9	5
4	5	9

9

Denver International SchoolHouse

Name:

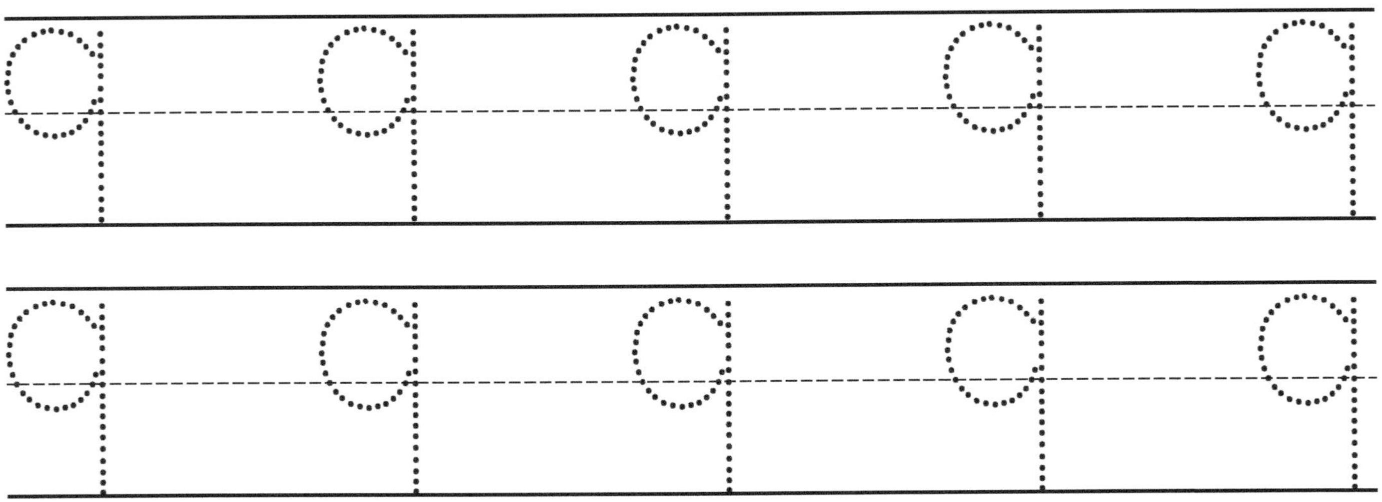

Color

Write

Search and color

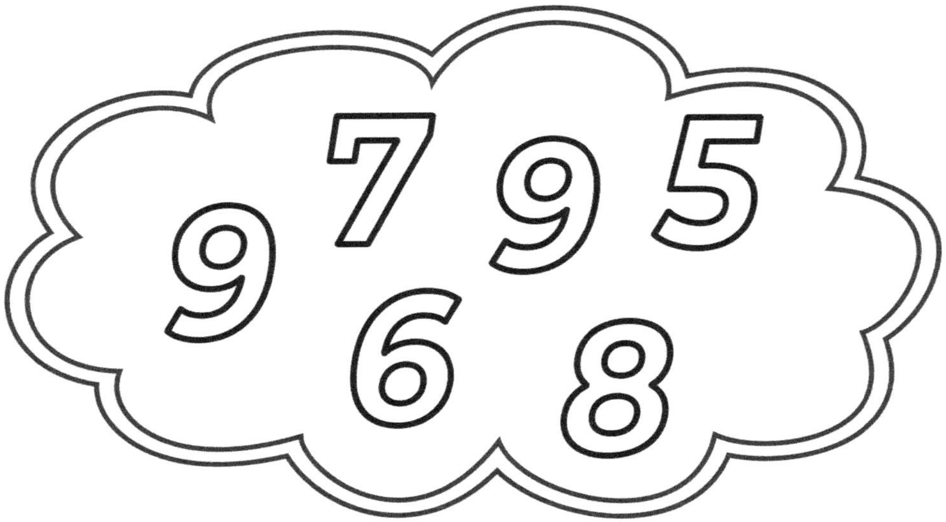

51

Denver International SchoolHouse

Name:_____

Nine

Trace. Use stickers to show the number.

Find the number 9. Subtract one and add one.

9 8 7 6 5 9
7 9 8 9 6 4

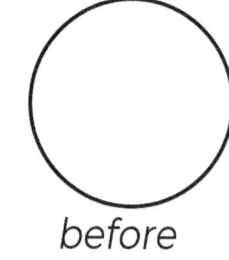  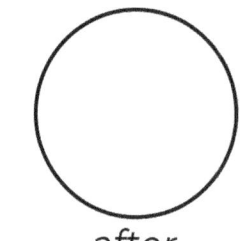
before after

Color the feathers according to the number.

Practice writing. Nine

Name:_____

Nine

Trace the number. Trace the number word.

9 9 9 9 9

Nine Nine

Nine Nine

Now, practice writing the number and the number word on your own.

Name:_____

Nine

Color nine apples.

Denver International SchoolHouse

Name:_____

Ten

Color the number 10. Color the 10 nuts.

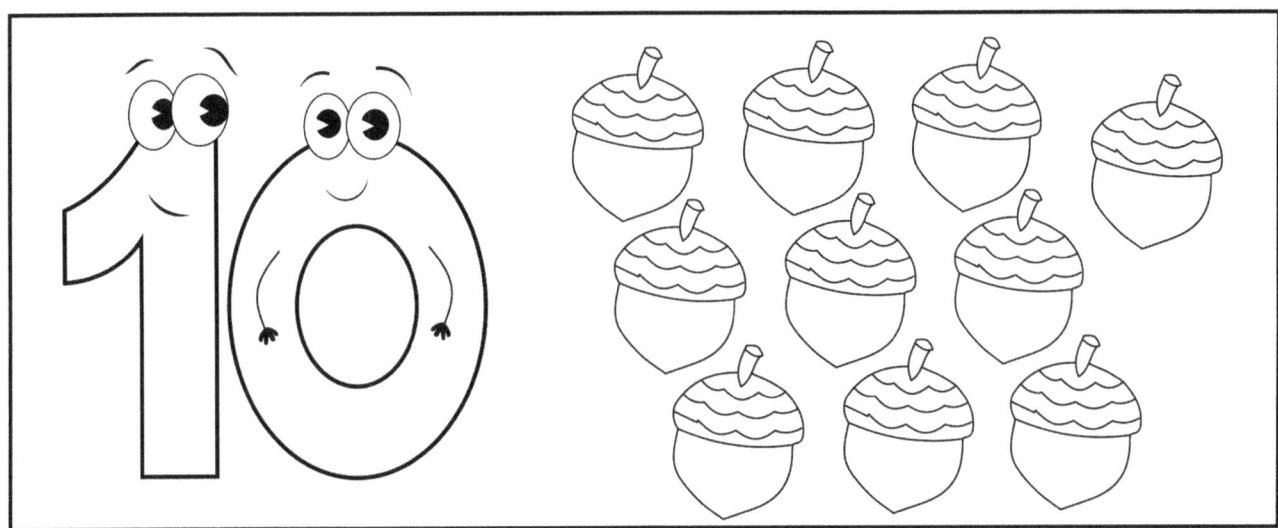

Trace the number 10.

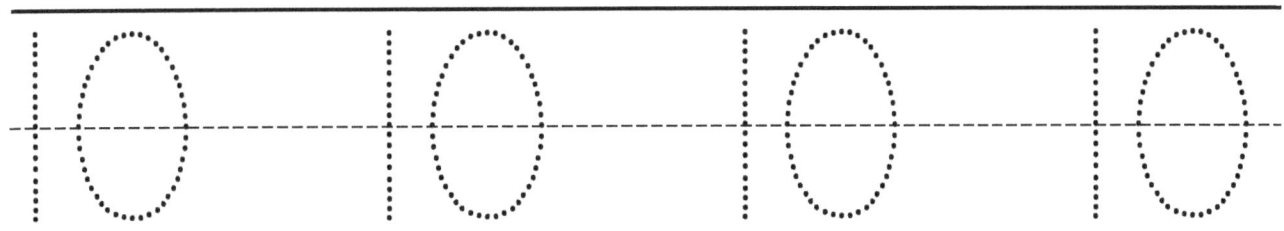

Circle the box showing 10.

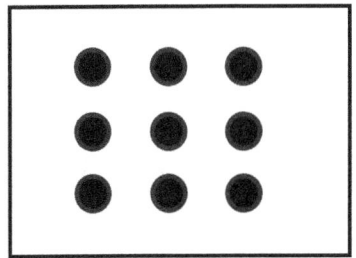 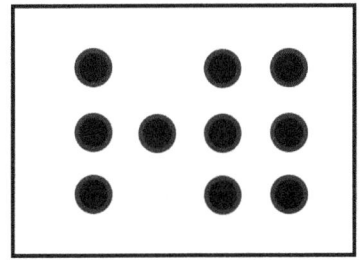 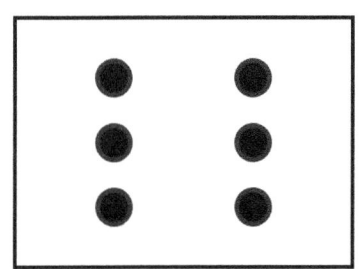

Name:_____

Ten

Color only the number 10.

1	5	10
10	3	11
6	10	5	9	2
10	13	4	10	6
7	10	5	**10**
10	5	13	

56   Denver International SchoolHouse

Name: _____

Color

Write

Search and color

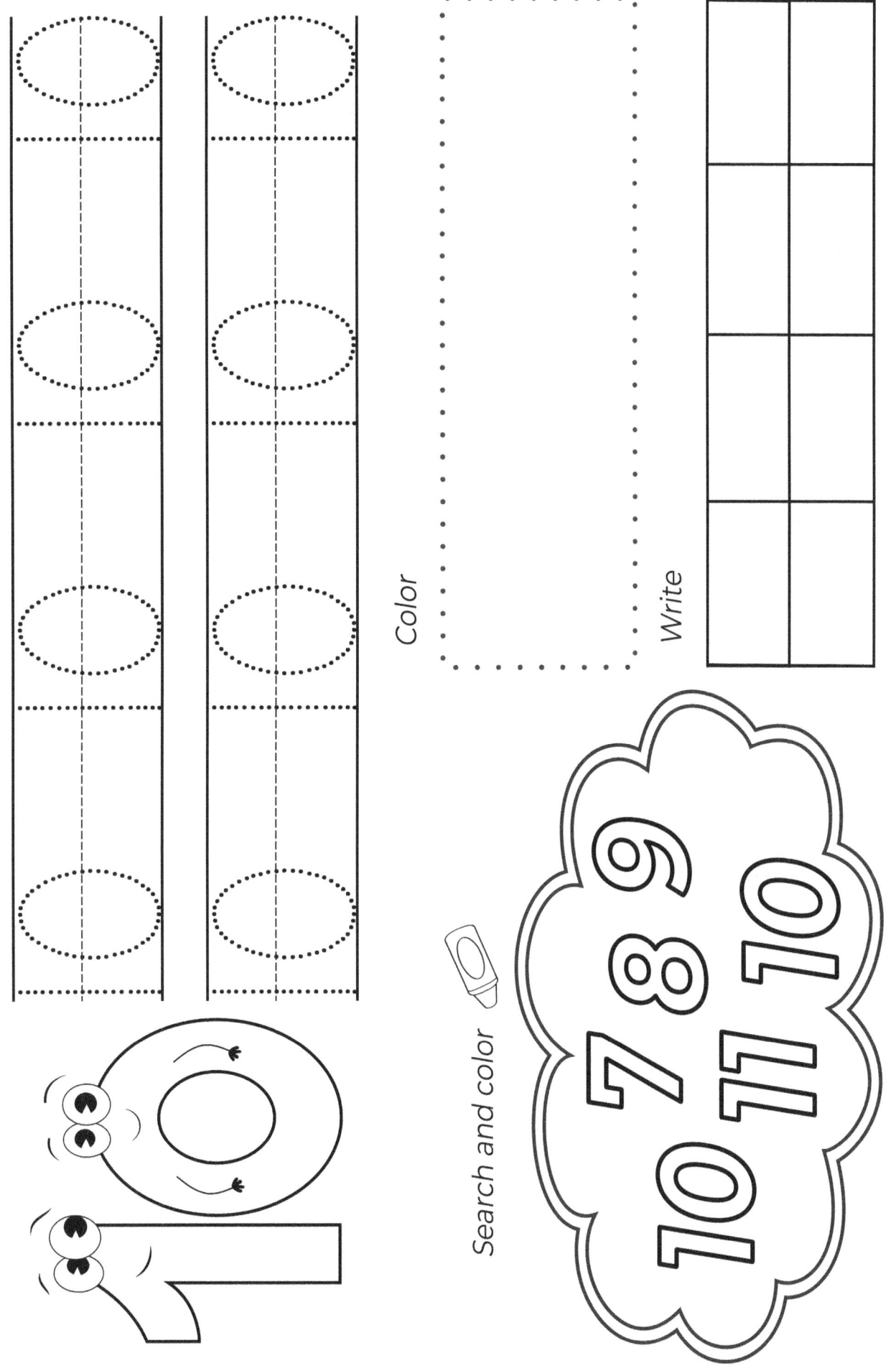

Name:_____

Ten

Trace.　　　　Use stickers to show the number.

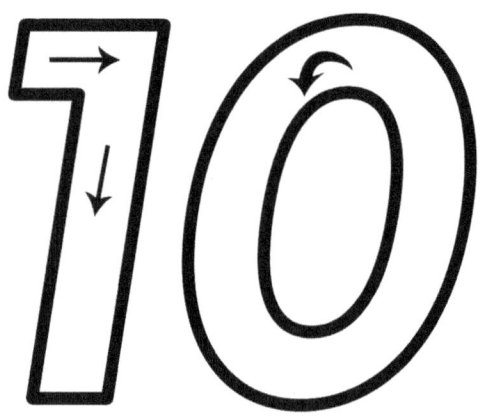

Find the number 10.　　　　Subtract one and add one.

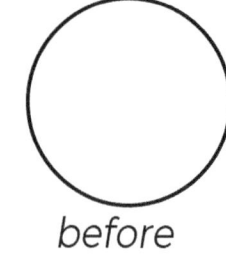
before

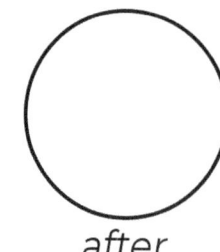
after

Color the feathers according to the number.

Practice writing.　　Ten　Ten

Name:_____

Ten

Trace the number. Trace the number word.

10 10 10 10

Ten Ten

Ten Ten

Now, practice writing the number and the number word on your own.

Name:_____

Ten

Color ten bees.

Name:_____

Eleven

Color the number 11. Color the 11 penguins.

Trace the number 11.

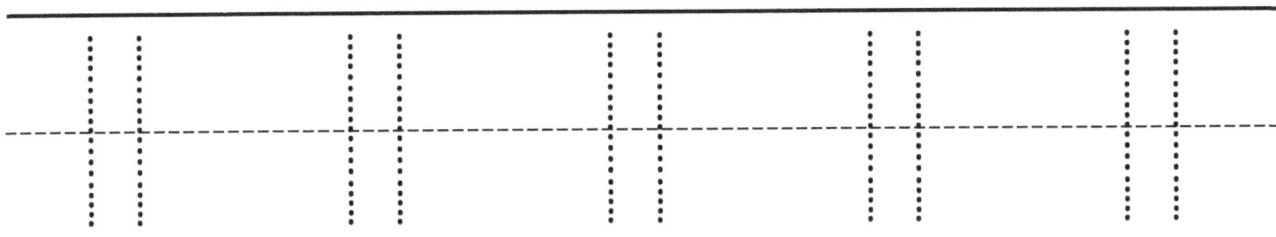

Circle the box showing 11.

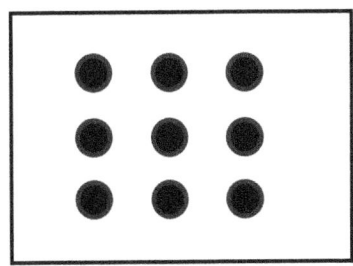 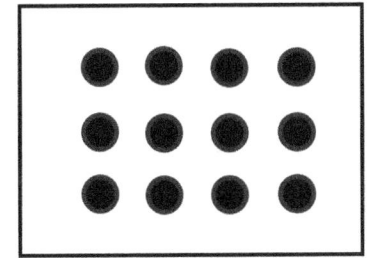 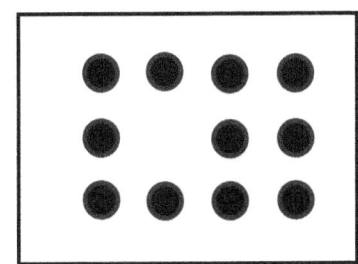

Name:_____

Eleven

Color only the number 11.

11	5	10
10	9	11

6	10	11	9	8
11	13	11	10	6

7	11	5
10	5	11

11

Denver International SchoolHouse

Name: _____

Color

Write

Search and color

Name:_____

Eleven

Trace.

Use stickers to show the number.

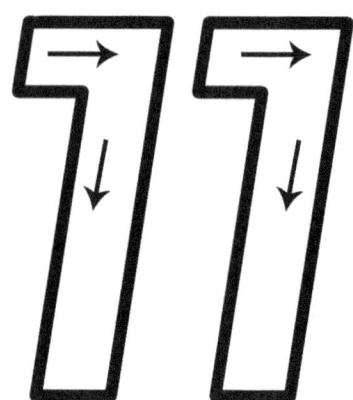

Find the number 11.

Subtract one and add one.

```
10  11  12  11  9  8
13  12  11  9  7  11
```

before

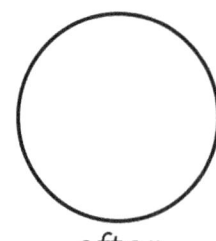

after

Color the feathers according to the number.

Practice writing.   Eleven

Denver International SchoolHouse

Name:_____

Eleven

Trace the number. Trace the number word.

11   11   11   11   11

Eleven

Eleven

Now, practice writing the number and the number word on your own.

Denver International SchoolHouse

Name:_____

Eleven

Color eleven butterflies.

Name:_____

Twelve

Color the number 12. Color the 12 fish.

Trace the number 12.

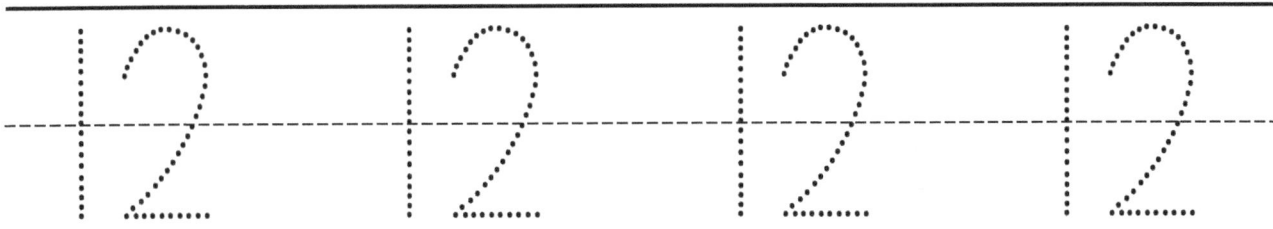

Circle the box showing 12.

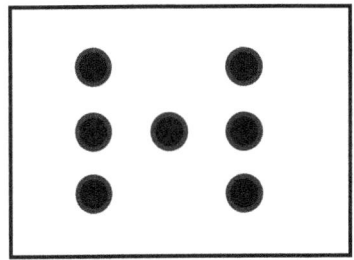 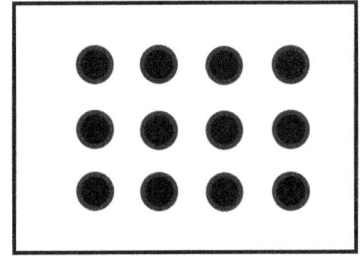 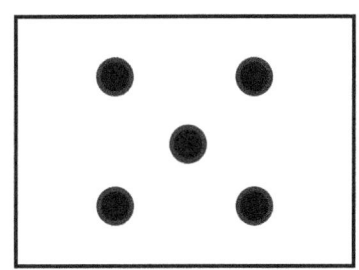

Name:_____

Twelve

Color only the number 12.

12	11	10
10	12	11
6	10	5	9	12
10	13	12	10	6
12	10	5
10	12	13

12

Denver International SchoolHouse

Name: _____

Color

Write

Search and color

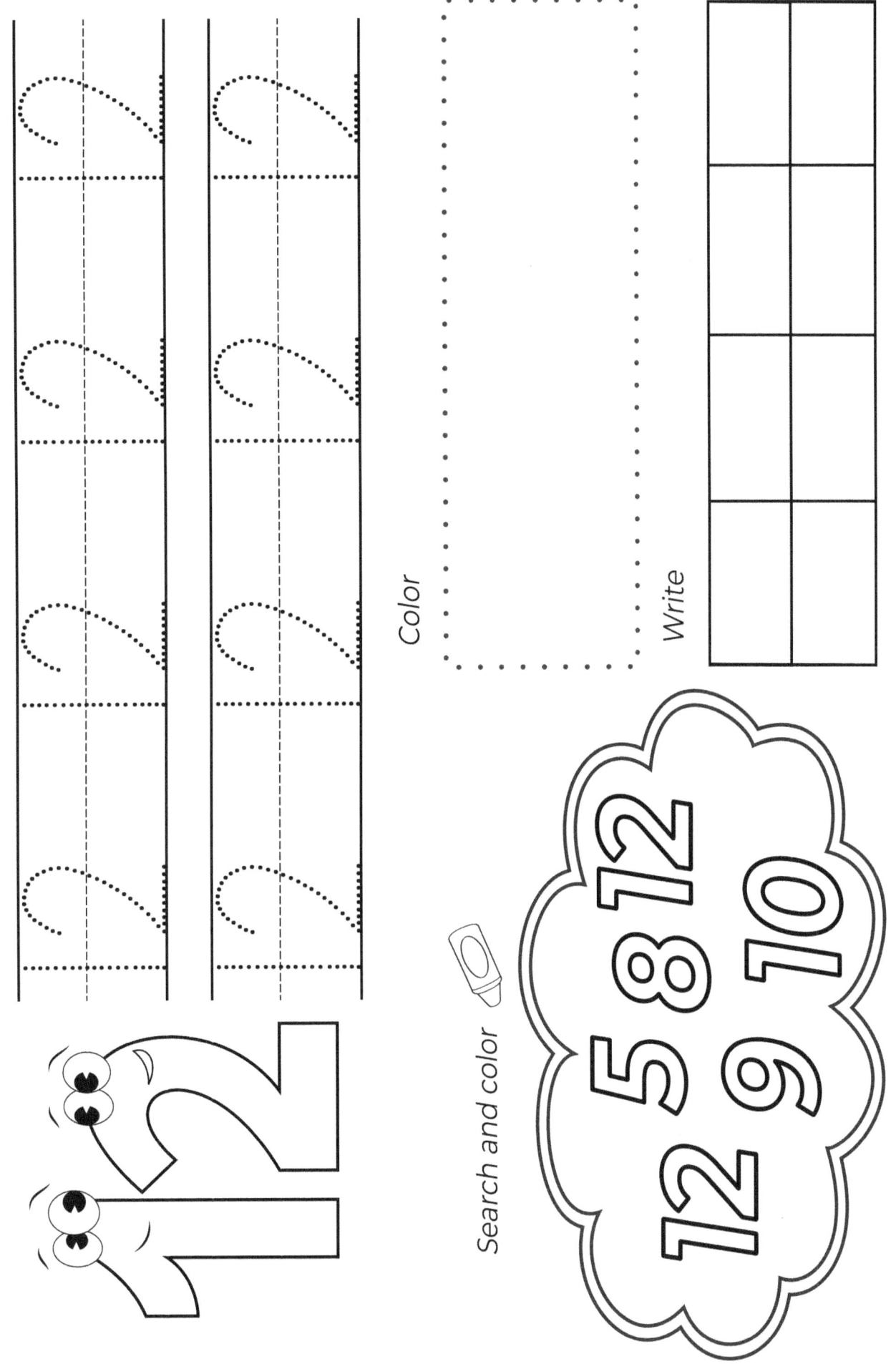

Name:_____

Twelve

Trace.

Use stickers to show the number.

Find the number 12.

12 10 11 9 7 6
11 14 12 13 12 2

Subtract one and add one.

before

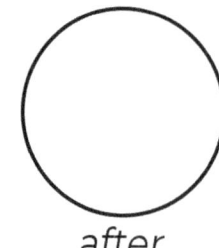
after

Color the feathers according to the number.

Practice writing.   Twelve

Name:_____

Twelve

Trace the number. Trace the number word.

12   12   12   12

Twelve

Twelve

Now, practice writing the number and the number word on your own.

Twelve

Name:_____

Color twelve ducks.

Denver International SchoolHouse

Name:_____

Thirteen

Color the number 13. Color the 13 pumpkins.

Trace the number 13.

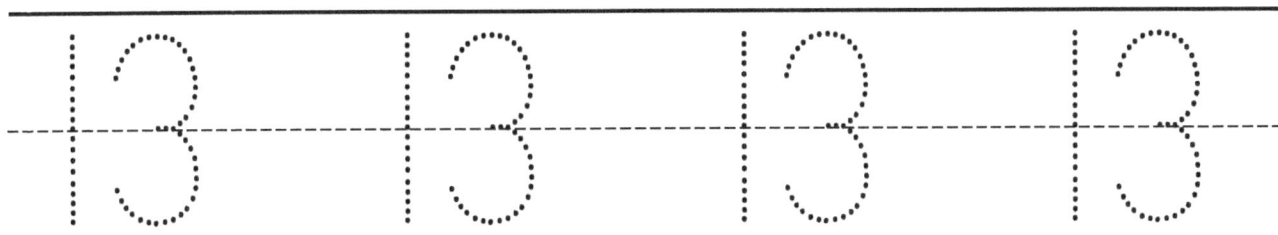

Circle the box showing 13.

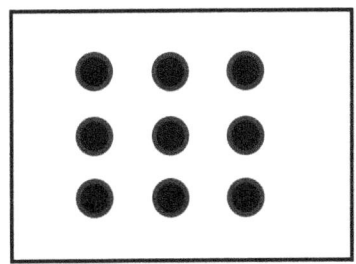   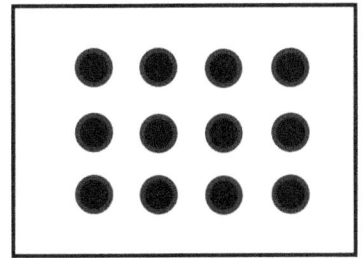   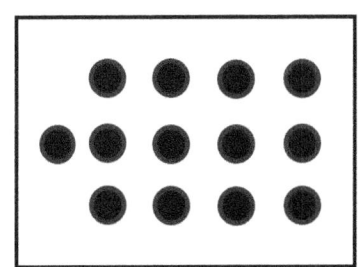

Name:_____

Thirteen

Color only the number 13.

12	13	10
10	13	11

13	10	5	9	12
10	13	13	10	6

12	13	5
10	12	13

13

Name: _____

Color

Write

Search and color

75 Denver International SchoolHouse

Name:_____

Thirteen

Trace.

Use stickers to show the number.

Find the number 13.

12 13 11 10 13 6
10 14 11 13 12 2

Subtract one and add one.

  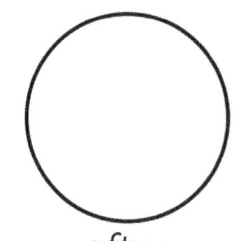

before　　　　　　　　after

Color the feathers according to the number.

Practice writing.　Thirteen

Denver International SchoolHouse　　76

Name:_____

Thirteen

Trace the number. Trace the number word.

13   13   13   13

Thirteen

Thirteen

Now, practice writing the number and the number word on your own.

Denver International SchoolHouse

Thirteen

Name:_____

Color thirteen balloons.

Name:_____

Fourteen

Color the number 14. Color the 14 drops.

Trace the number 14.

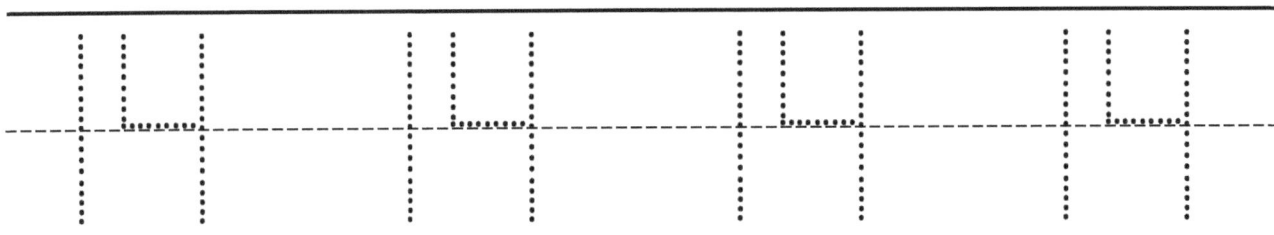

Circle the box showing 14.

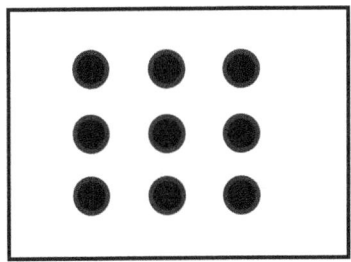 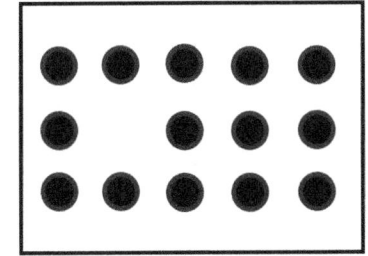 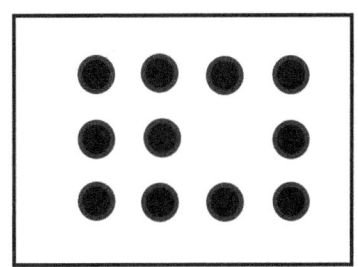

Name:_____

Fourteen

Color only the number 14.

14	13	10
10	14	11
15	14	11	9	16
11	13	14	10	14
14	13	5	
13	5	14	**14**

Denver International SchoolHouse

Name: _____

Color

Write

Search and color

Name:_____

Fourteen

Trace.

Use stickers to show the number.

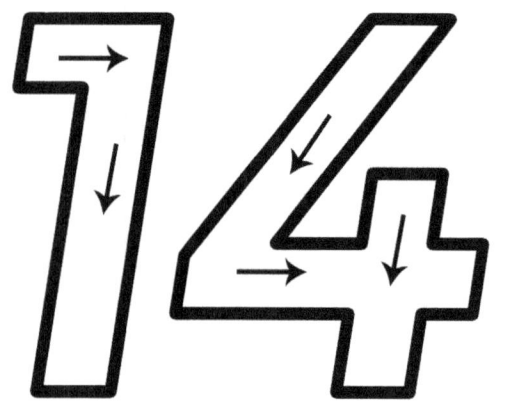

Find the number 14.

10 14 12 13 9 7
14 12 14 9 7 11

Subtract one and add one.

  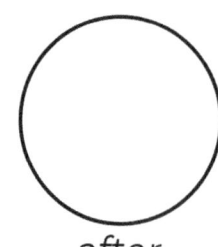

before   after

Color the feathers according to the number.

Practice writing.

Name:_____

Fourteen

Trace the number. Trace the number word.

14   14   14   14

Fourteen

Fourteen

Now, practice writing the number and the number word on your own.

Name:_____

Fourteen

Color fourteen flowers.

Name:_____

Fifteen

Color the number 15. Color the 15 balloons.

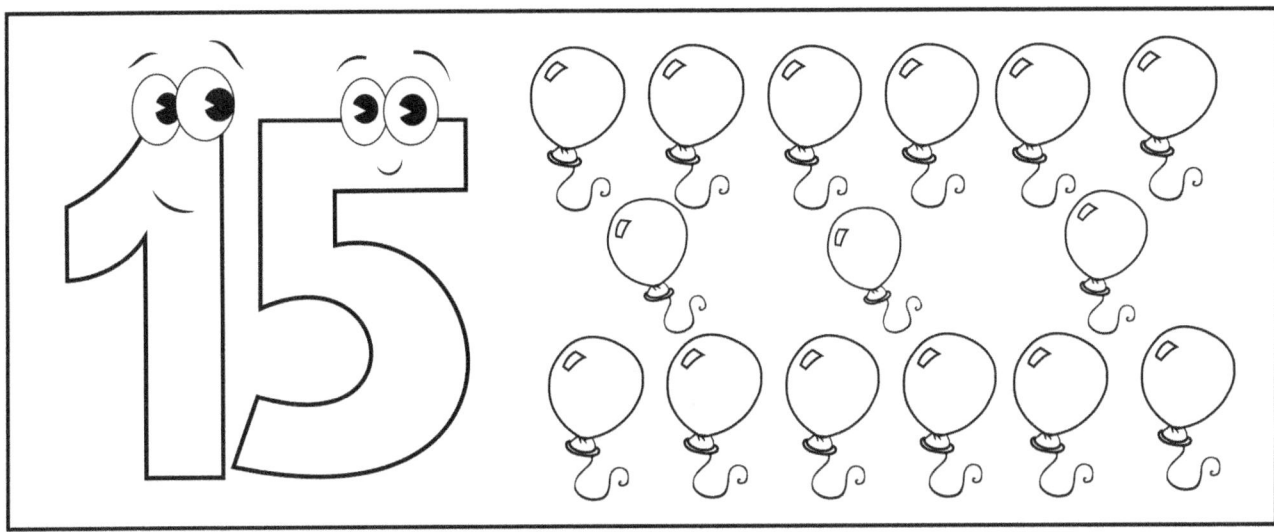

Trace the number 15.

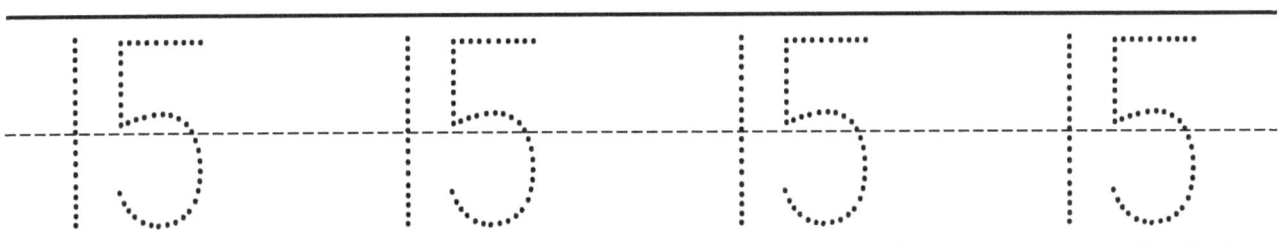

Circle the box showing 15.

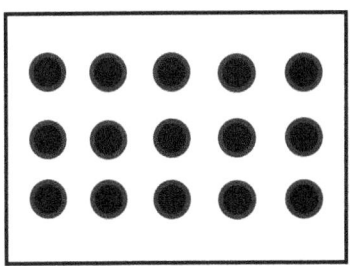 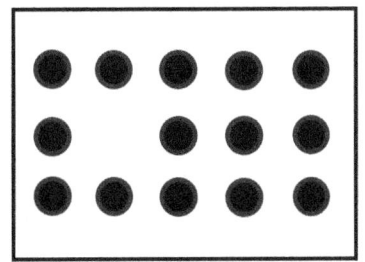 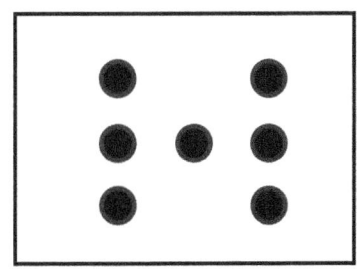

Name:_____

Fifteen

Color only the number 15.

		12	11	15
		10	15	16
6	10	15	9	12
10	15	12	10	15
16	10	15		
15	12	13	**15**	

Denver International SchoolHouse

Name: _____

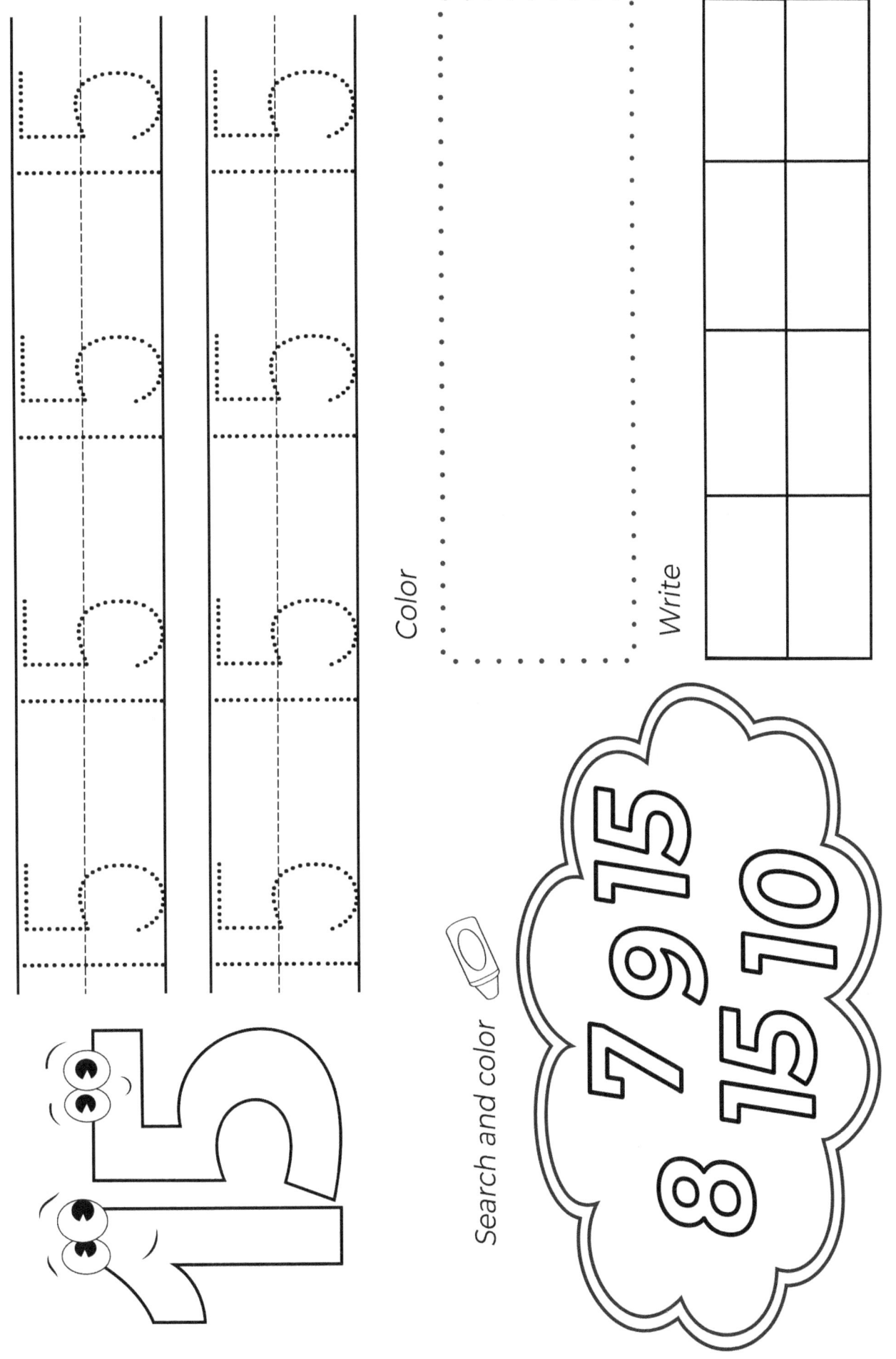

Color

Write

Search and color

Name:_____

Fifteen

Trace.

Use stickers to show the number.

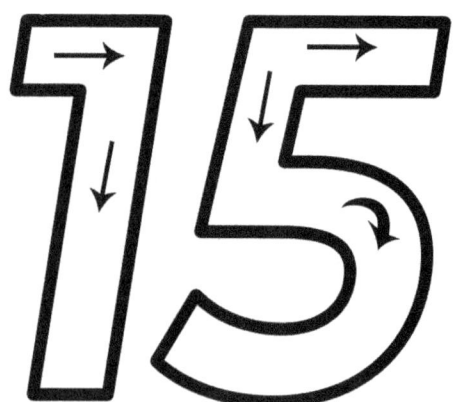

Find the number 15.

Subtract one and add one.

15 16 14 10 12
13 15 14 15 16

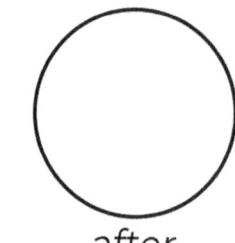

before   after

Color the feathers according to the number.

Practice writing. Fifteen

Name:_____

Fifteen

Trace the number. Trace the number word.

15   15   15   15

Fifteen

Fifteen

Now, practice writing the number and the number word on your own.

Name:_____

Fifteen

Color fifteen candies.

Name:_____

Sixteen

Color the number 16. Color the 16 bows.

Trace the number 16.

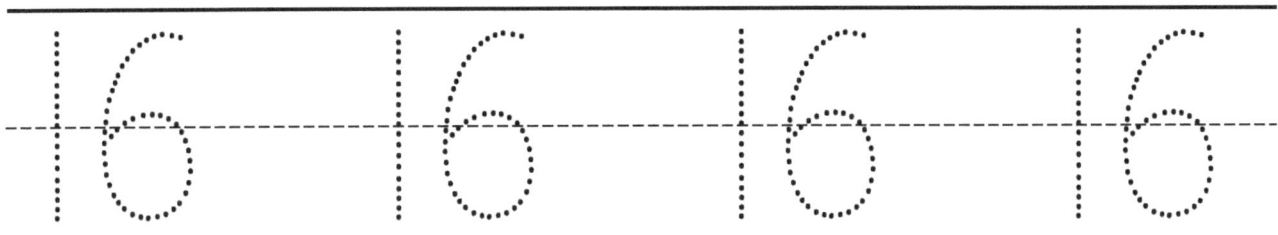

Circle the box showing 16.

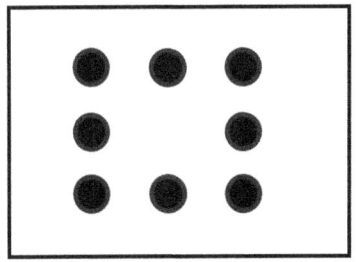 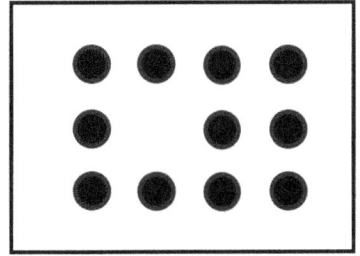 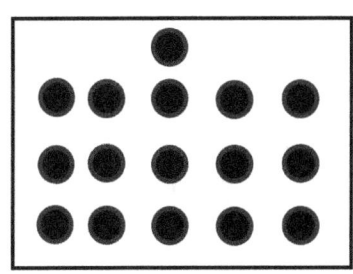

Name:_____

Sixteen

Color only the number 16.

16	13	15
17	13	16
16	10	16	9	12
19	16	13	10	6
12	13	16	**16**
10	16	13	

Denver International SchoolHouse

Name:_____

Color

Write

Search and color

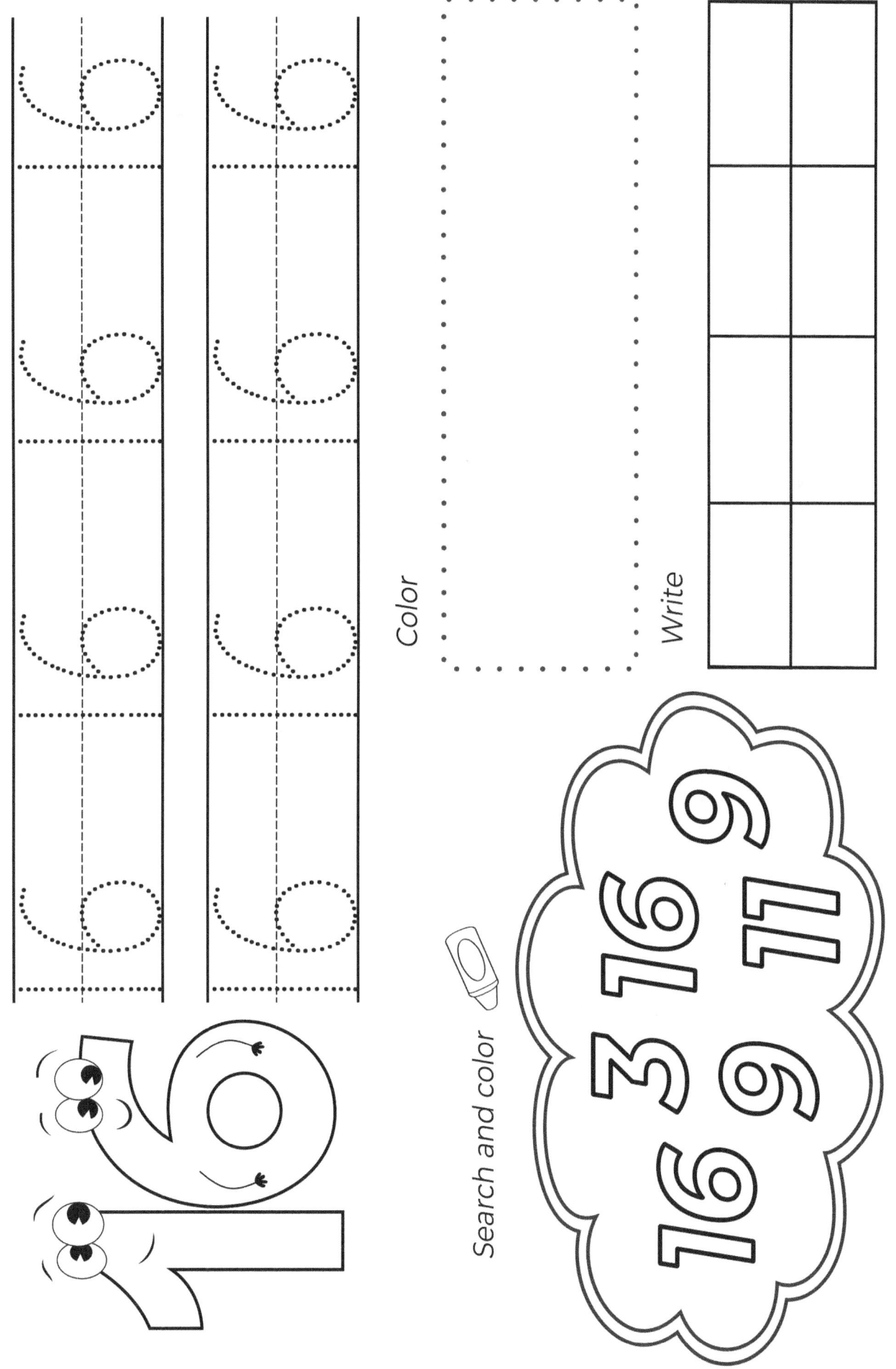

Name:_____

Sixteen

Trace. Use stickers to show the number.

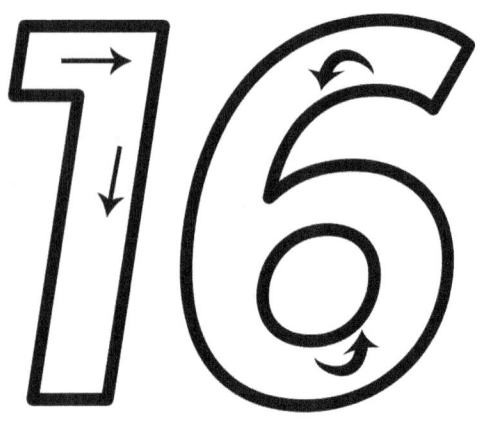 

Find the number 16. Subtract one and add one.

15 14 16 12 16
16 14 15 13 12

  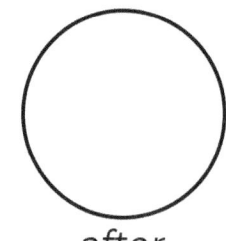

before   after

Color the feathers according to the number.

Practice writing.   Sixteen

Name:_____

Sixteen

Trace the number. Trace the number word.

16 16 16 16

Sixteen

Sixteen

Now, practice writing the number and the number word on your own.

95   Denver International SchoolHouse

Sixteen

Name:_____

Color sixteen gifts.

Name:_____

Seventeen

Color the number 17. Color the 17 popsicles.

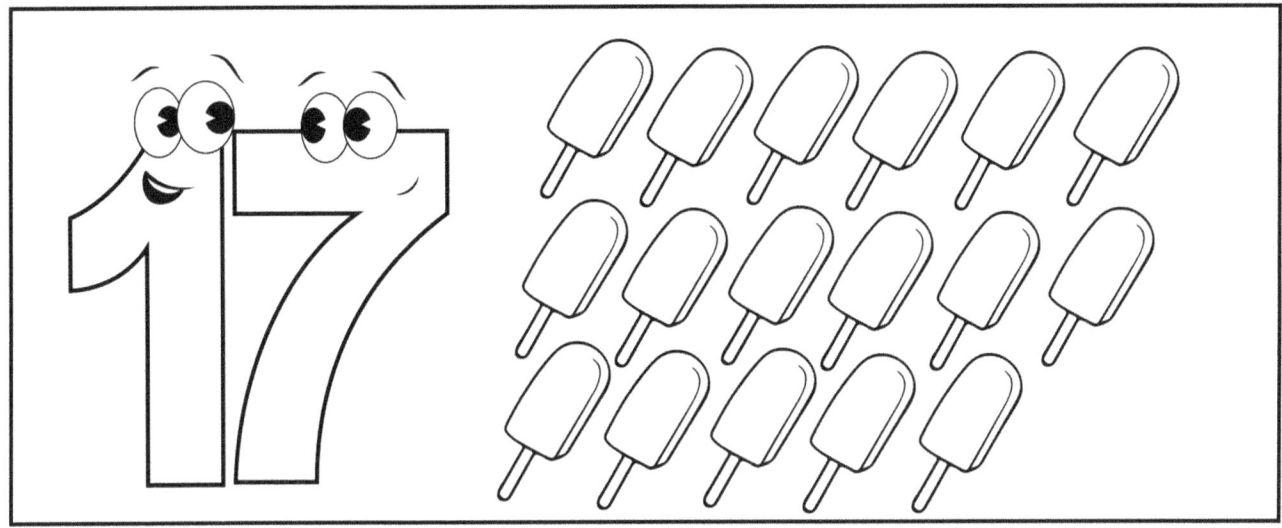

Trace the number 17.

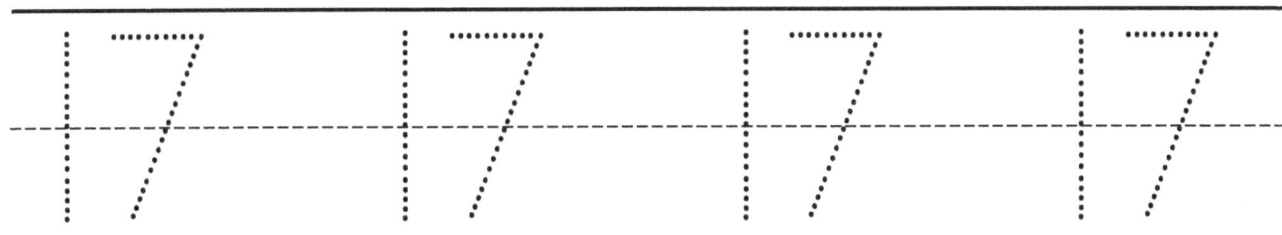

Circle the box showing 17.

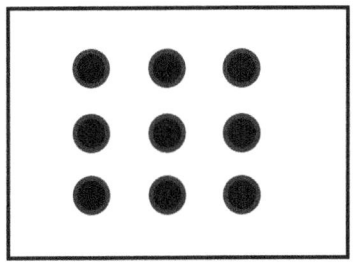 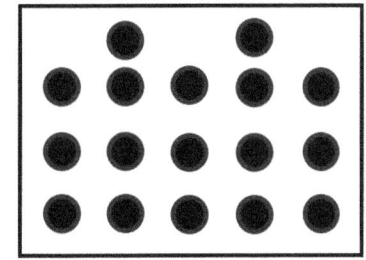 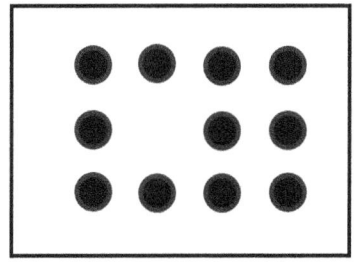

Name:_____

Seventeen

Color only the number 17.

11	17	10
17	9	11

6	10	11	17	8
11	17	11	10	17

7	11	17
17	5	11

17

Denver International SchoolHouse 98

Name: _____

Color

Write

Search and color

99

Denver International SchoolHouse

Name:_____

Seventeen

Trace.

Use stickers to show the number.

Find the number 17.

17 16 15 14 13
14 17 15 17 16

Subtract one and add one.

before   after

Color the feathers according to the number.

Practice writing.   Seventeen

Denver International SchoolHouse

Name:_____

Seventeen

Trace the number. Trace the number word.

17 17 17 17

Seventeen

Seventeen

Now, practice writing the number and the number word on your own.

Name:_____

Seventeen

Color seventeen stars.

Name:_____

Eighteen

Color the number 18. Color the 18 ice cream cones.

Trace the number 18.

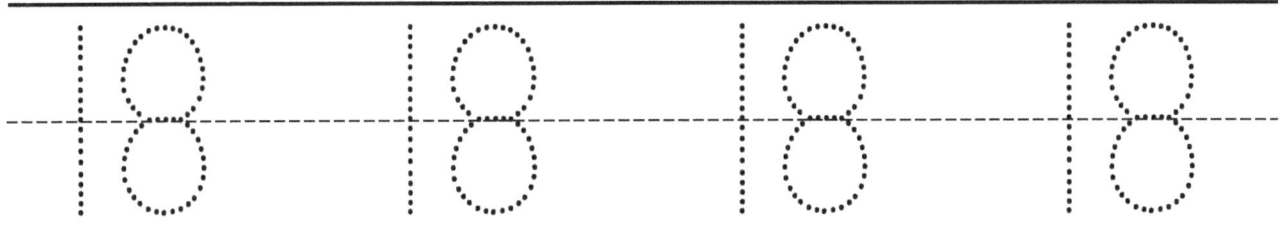

Circle the box showing 18.

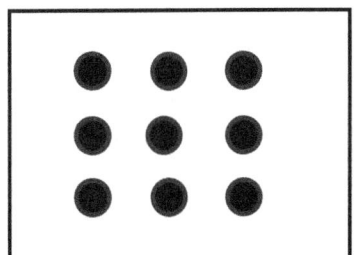 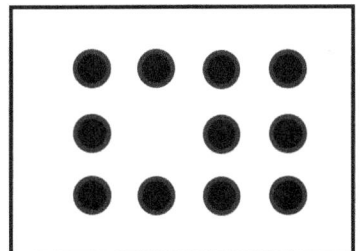 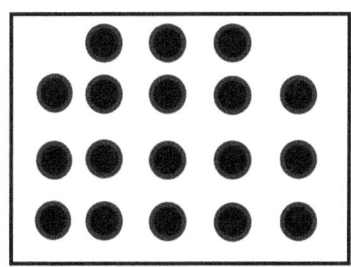

Name:_____

Eighteen

Color only the number 18.

| 18 | 13 | 15 |
| 17 | 18 | 16 |

| 16 | 18 | 16 | 9 | 18 |
| 19 | 16 | 13 | 18 | 6 |

| 12 | 18 | 16 |
| 18 | 16 | 13 |

18

Denver International SchoolHouse

Name:_____

Color

Write

Search and color

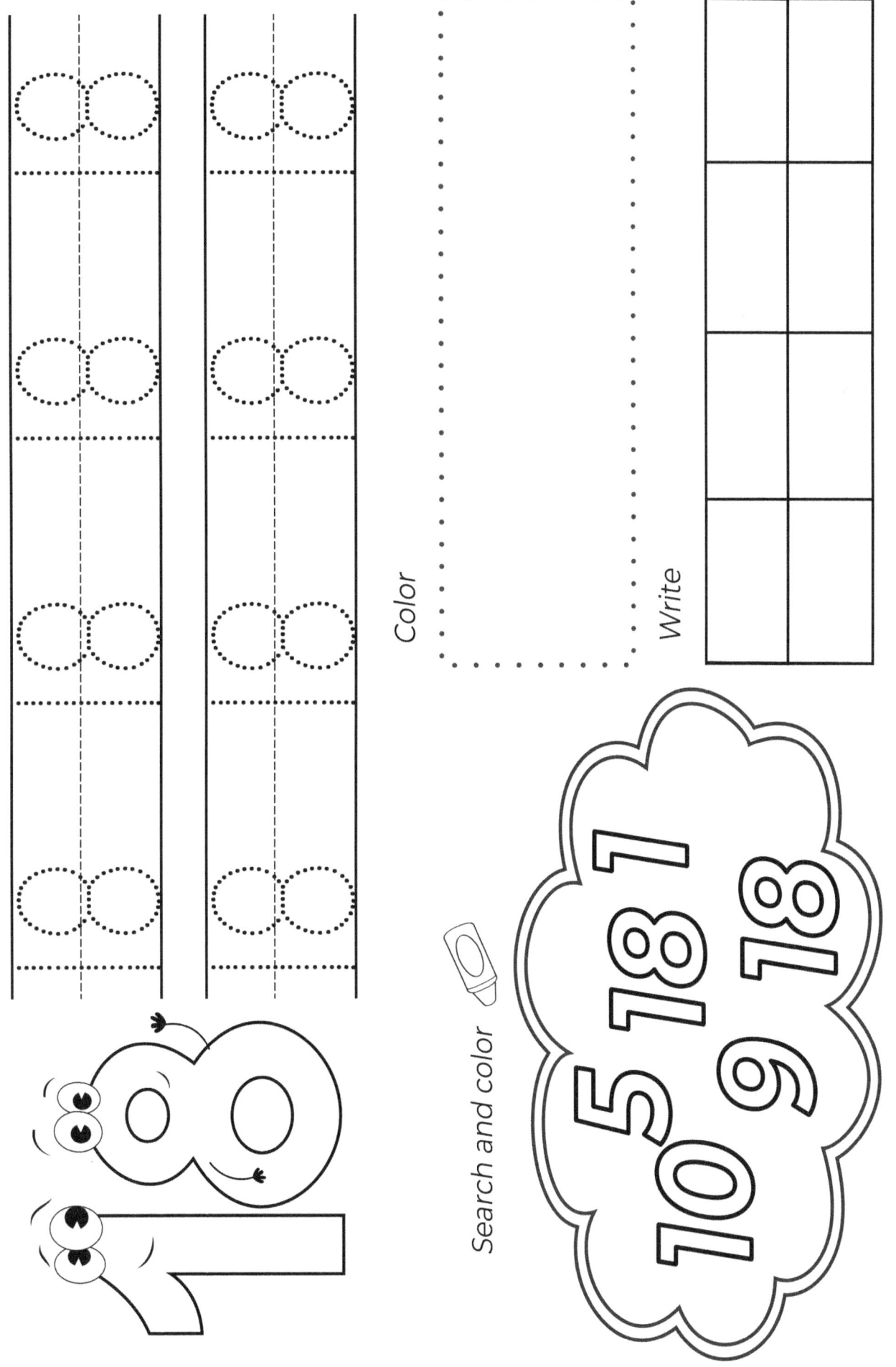

Name:_____

Eighteen

Trace. Use stickers to show the number.

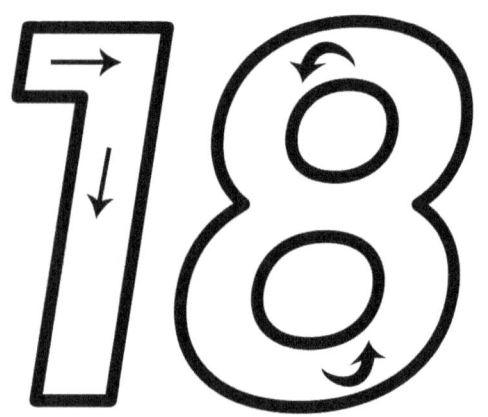

Find the number 18. Subtract one and add one.

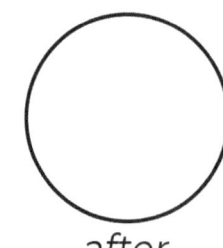

before   after

Color the feathers according to the number.

Practice writing. Eighteen

Name:_____

Eighteen

Trace the number. Trace the number word.

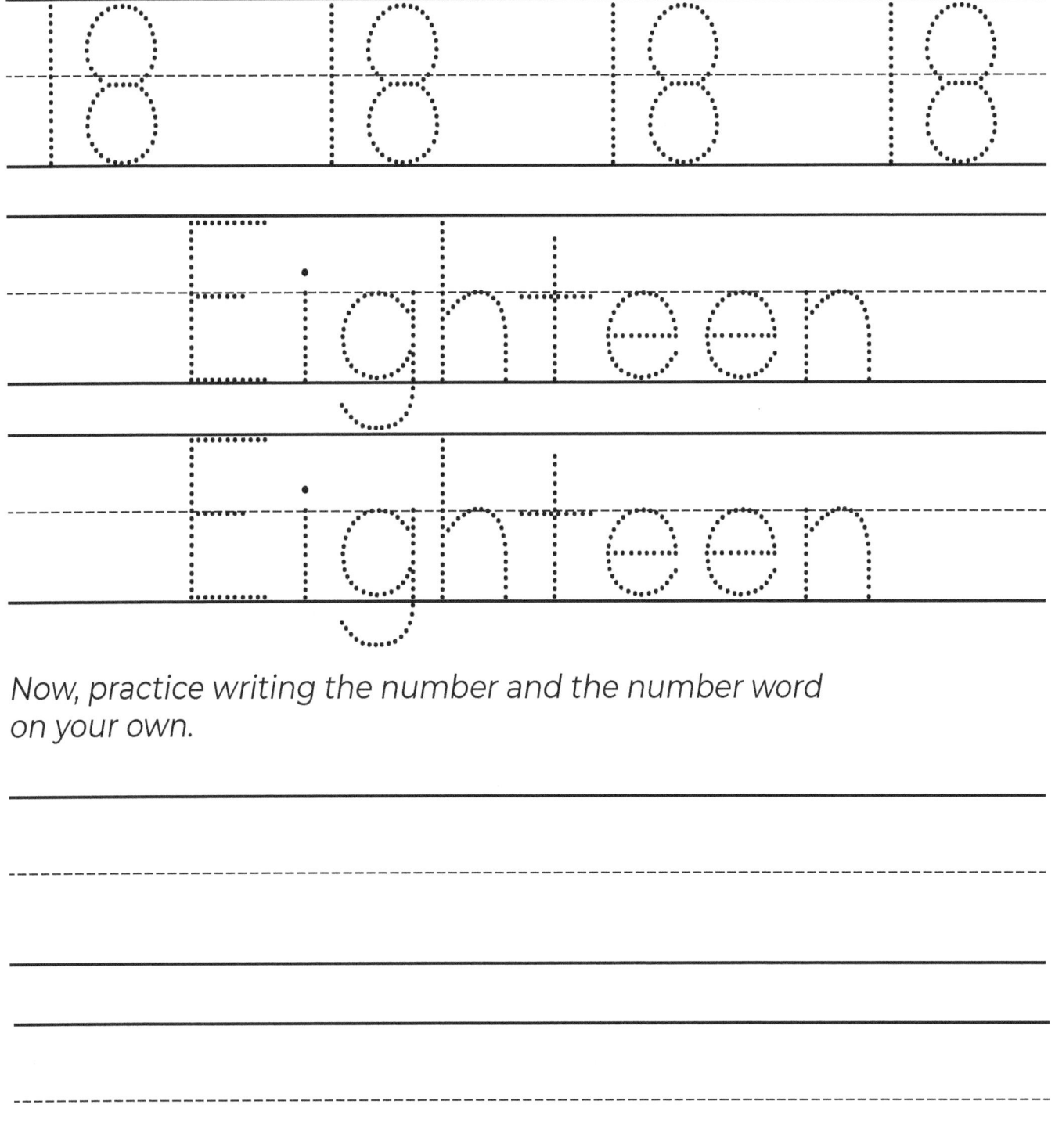

Now, practice writing the number and the number word on your own.

Name:_____

Eighteen

Color eighteen soldiers.

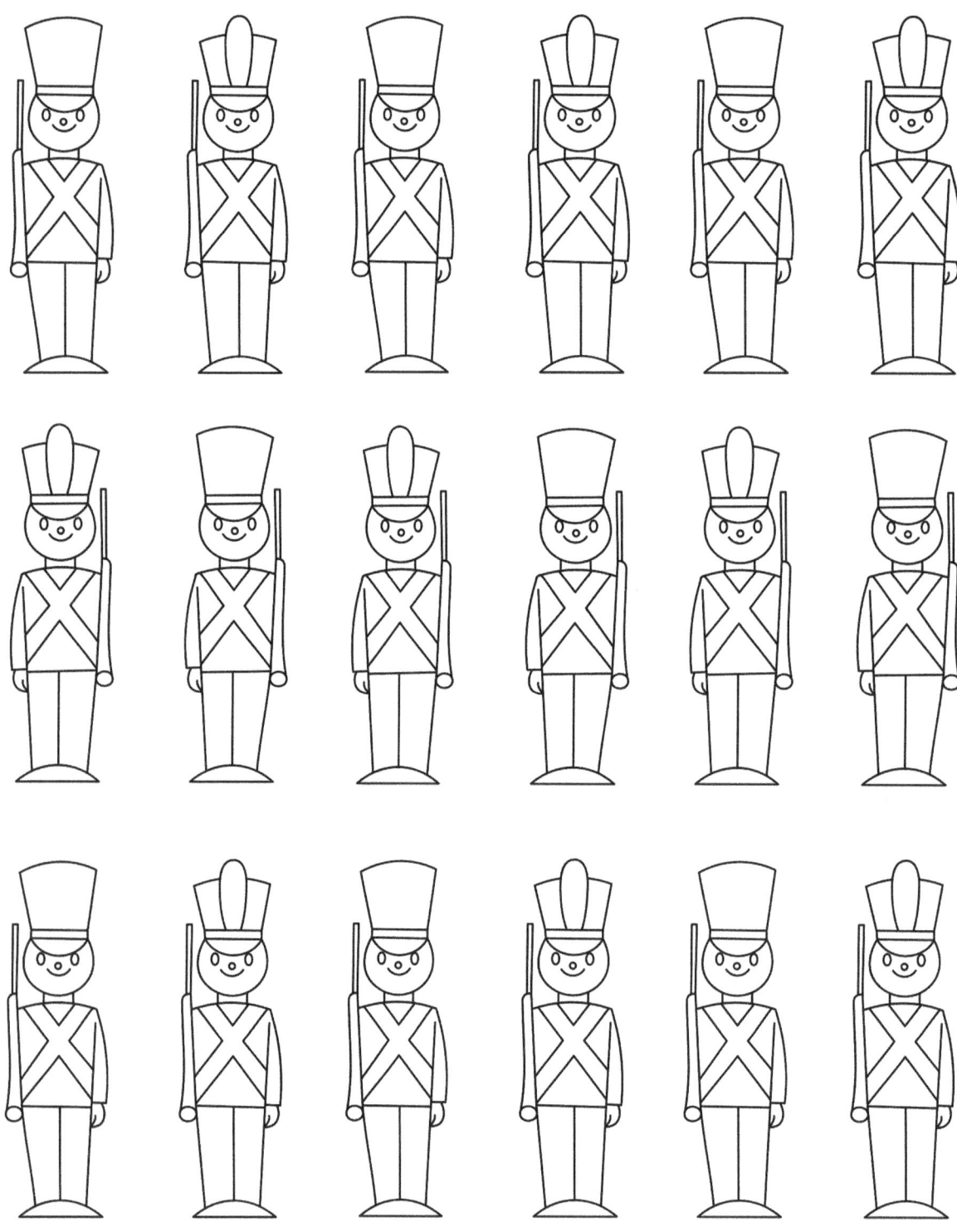

Name:_____

Nineteen

Color the number 19. Color the 19 hats.

Trace the number 19.

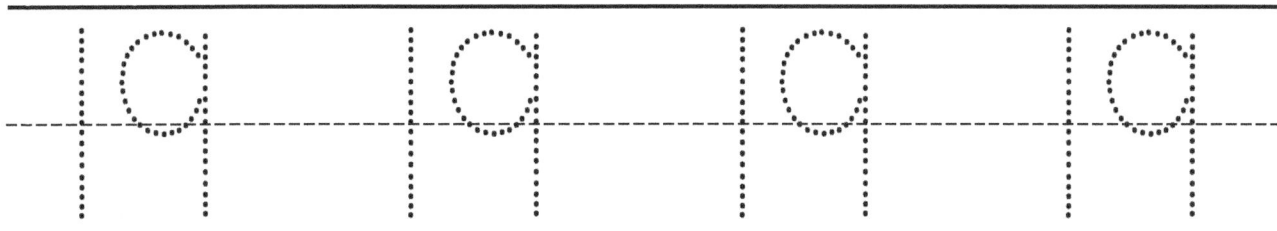

Circle the box showing 19.

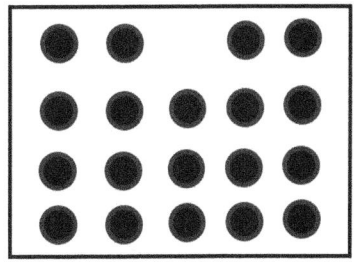
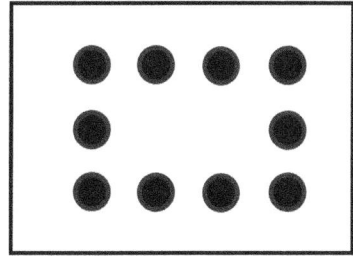
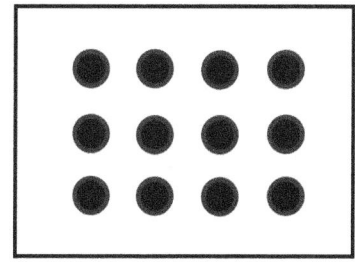

Name:_____

Nineteen

Color only the number 19.

18	19	15
15	19	16
13	14	19	19	18
19	16	13	9	6
12	18	19		
19	16	13		

19

Denver International SchoolHouse

Name:_____

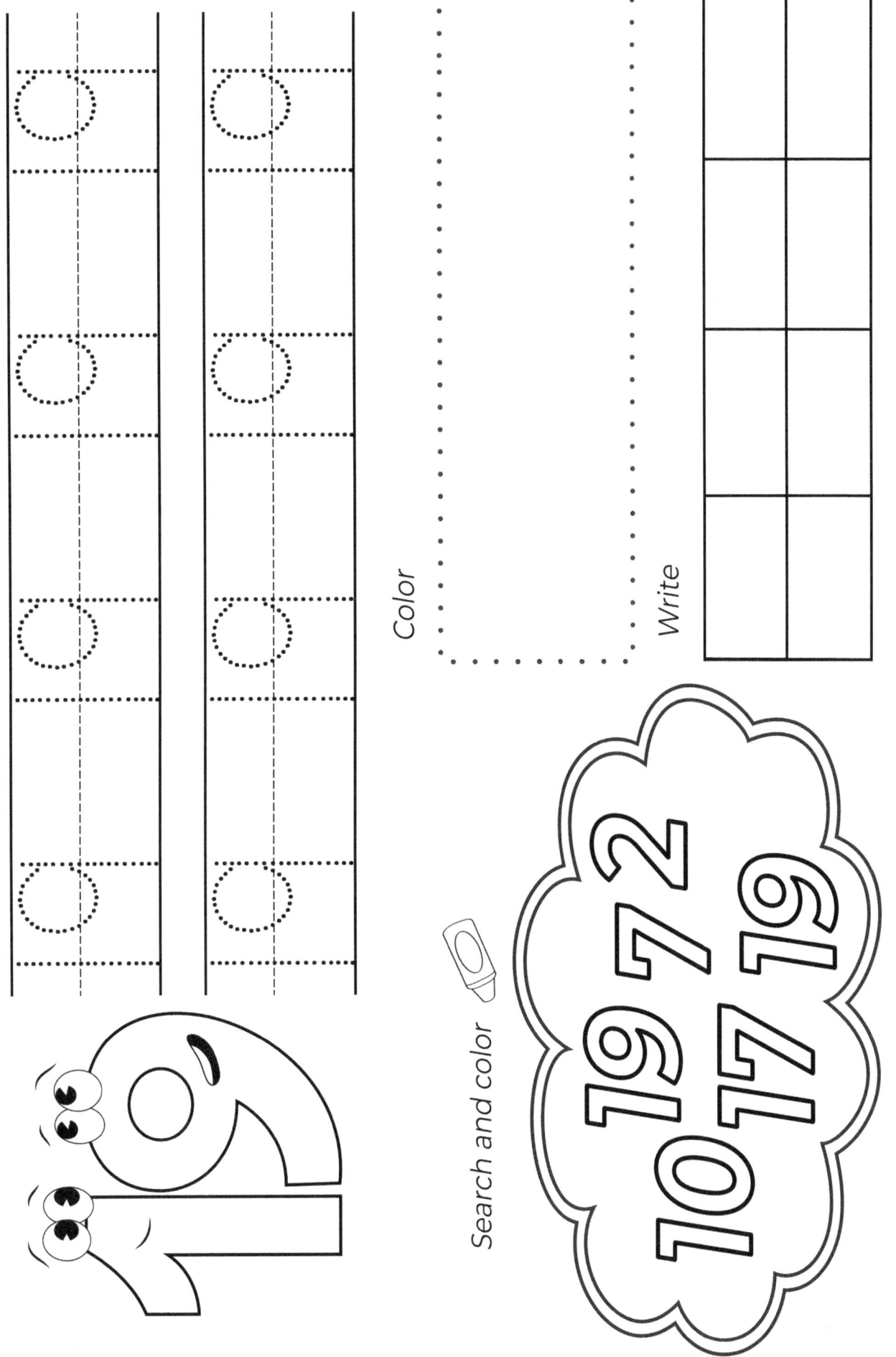

Color

Write

Search and color

Name:_____

Nineteen

Trace.   Use stickers to show the number.

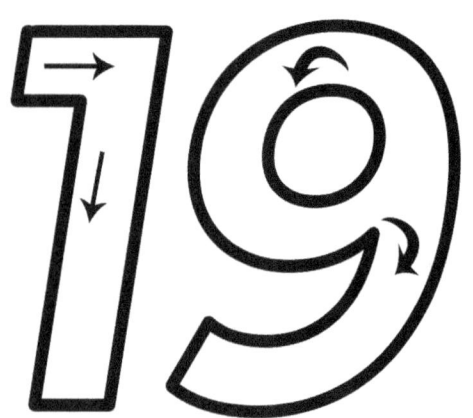

Find the number 19.   Subtract one and add one.

18 19 17 16 19
19 18 17 16 15

  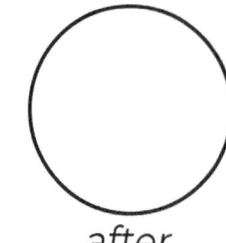

before   after

Color the feathers according to the number.

Practice writing.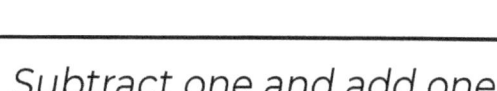

Name:_____

Nineteen

Trace the number. Trace the number word.

19   19   19   19   19

Nineteen

Nineteen

Now, practice writing the number and the number word on your own.

113 Denver International SchoolHouse

Name:_____

Nineteen

Color 19 Christmas ornaments

Name:_____

Twenty

Color the number 20. Color the 20 bees.

Trace the number 20.

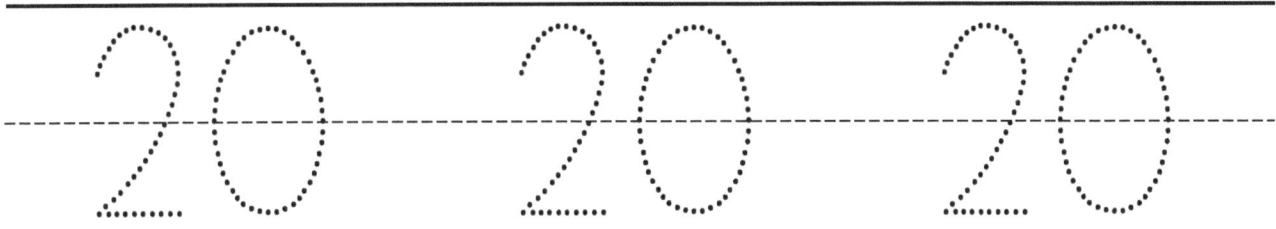

Circle the box showing 20.

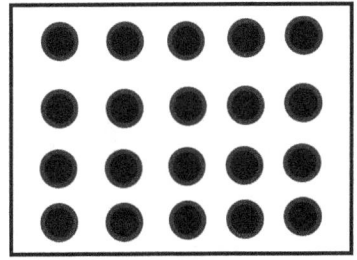 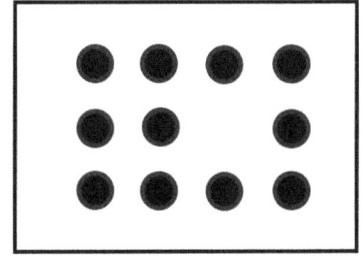 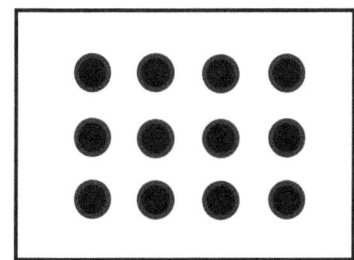

Name:_____

Twenty

Color only the number 20.

	18	19	20
	20	19	16
13	14	19	20	18
19	20	13	9	20
20	18	19		
19	20	13	**20**	

Name: _____

Color

Write

Search and color

117 Denver International SchoolHouse

Name:_____

Twenty

Trace. Use stickers to show the number.

Find the number 20. Subtract one and add one.

18 20 17 20 19
19 18 17 20 15

      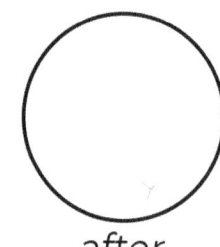

before   after

Color the feathers according to the number.

Practice writing.   Twenty

Denver International SchoolHouse   118

Name:_____

Twenty

Trace the number. Trace the number word.

20 20 20

Twenty

Twenty

Now, practice writing the number and the number word on your own.

Name:_____

Twenty

Color 20 candles.

Denver International SchoolHouse

Numbers 1-10

1	2	3	4	5	6	7	8	9	10
1	2	3	4	5	6	7	8	9	10
1	2	3	4	5	6	7	8	9	10
1	2	3	4	5	6	7	8	9	10
1	2	3	4	5	6	7	8	9	10
1	2	3	4	5	6	7	8	9	10
1	2	3	4	5	6	7	8	9	10

Denver International SchoolHouse

Name:_____

Number review

Count and color. Circle how many.

Numbers 11-20

11	12	13	14	15	16	17	18	19	20
11	12	13	14	15	16	17	18	19	20
11	12	13	14	15	16	17	18	19	20
11	12	13	14	15	16	17	18	19	20
11	12	13	14	15	16	17	18	19	20
11	12	13	14	15	16	17	18	19	20
11	12	13	14	15	16	17	18	19	20
11	12	13	14	15	16	17	18	19	20
11	12	13	14	15	16	17	18	19	20

Denver International SchoolHouse

Name:_____

Number review

Circle the group with the most.

 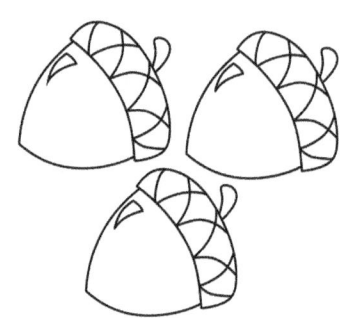

 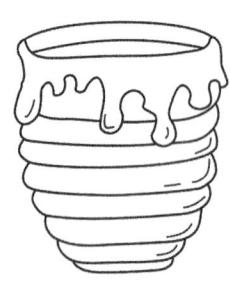

Name:_____

Number review

Circle the group with the least.

Number review

Name:_____

Count. Write how many there are in all.

Total

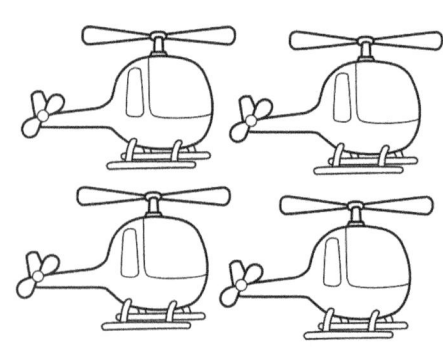  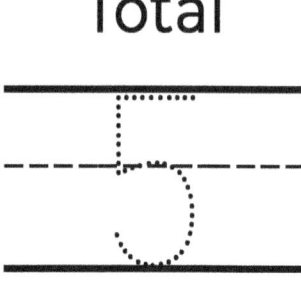

  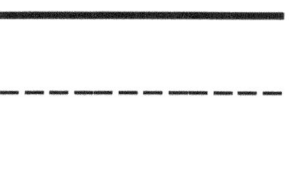

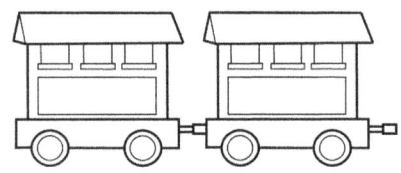 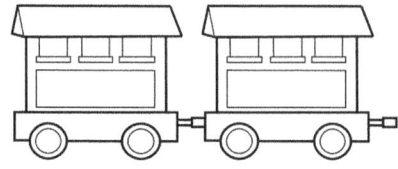

Denver International SchoolHouse

Number review

Name:_____

Count. Write how many there are in all.

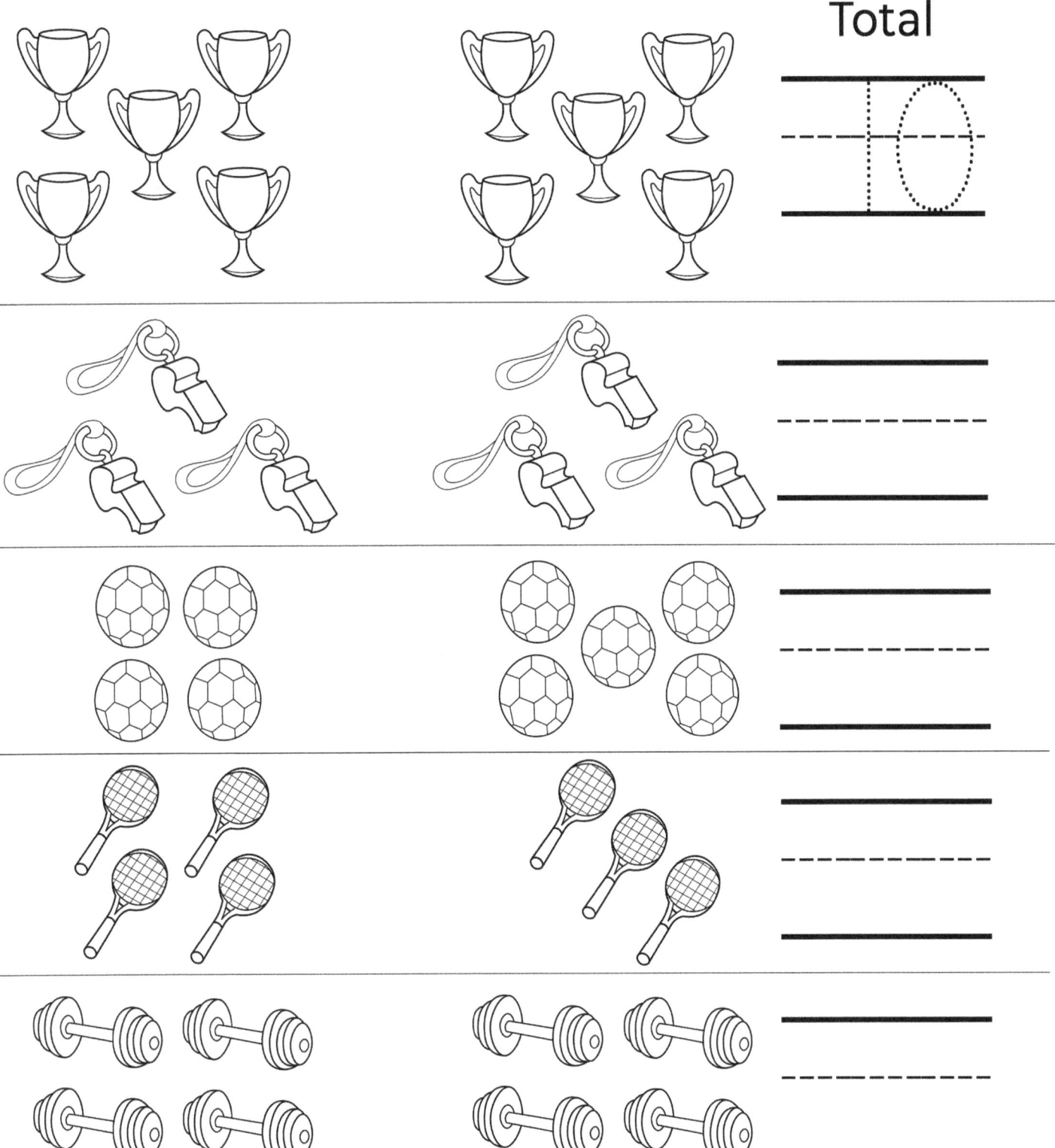

Name:_____

Number review

Add. Write how many there are in all.

    3   +   0   =   3

 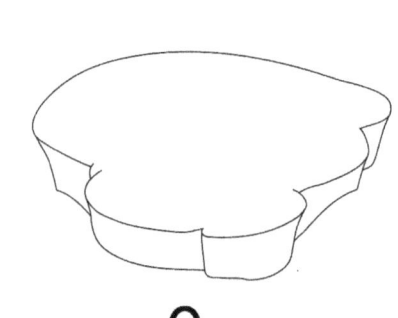

    4   +   0   =   Total _____

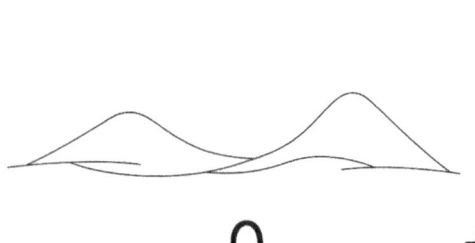 

    0   +   2   =   Total _____

    2   +   0   =   Total _____

Denver International SchoolHouse

Number review

Name:_____

Match.

3 three

1 one

2 two

4 four

Name:_____

Number review

Use the number to color the image.

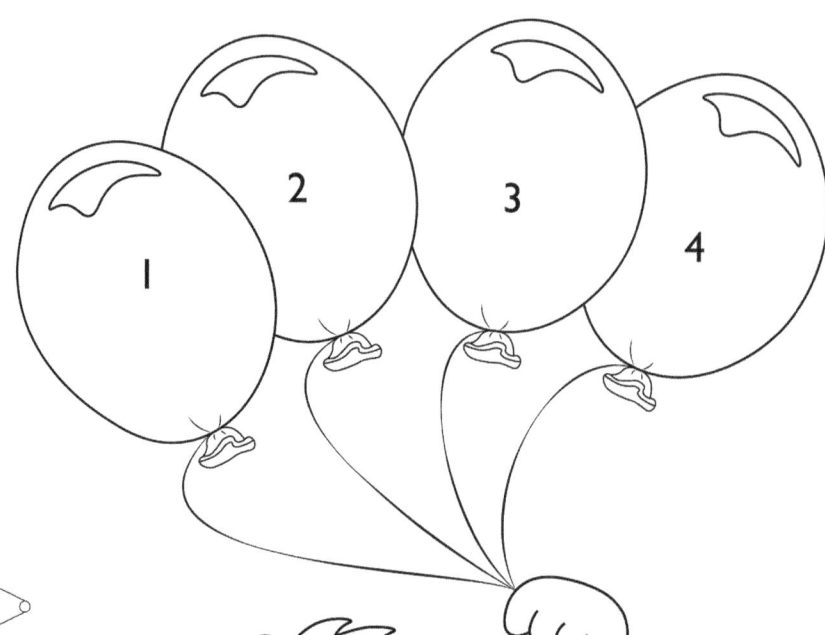

1 = blue

2 = red

3 = yellow

4 = pink

5 = brown

Name:_____

Number review

Use the number to color the image.

1 = gray   2 = orange   3 = green

4 = red   5 = pink

131   Denver International SchoolHouse

Name:_____

Number review

Match.

   6 six

   5 five

   7 seven

   4 four

Name:_____

Number review

Connect the dots 1-20.

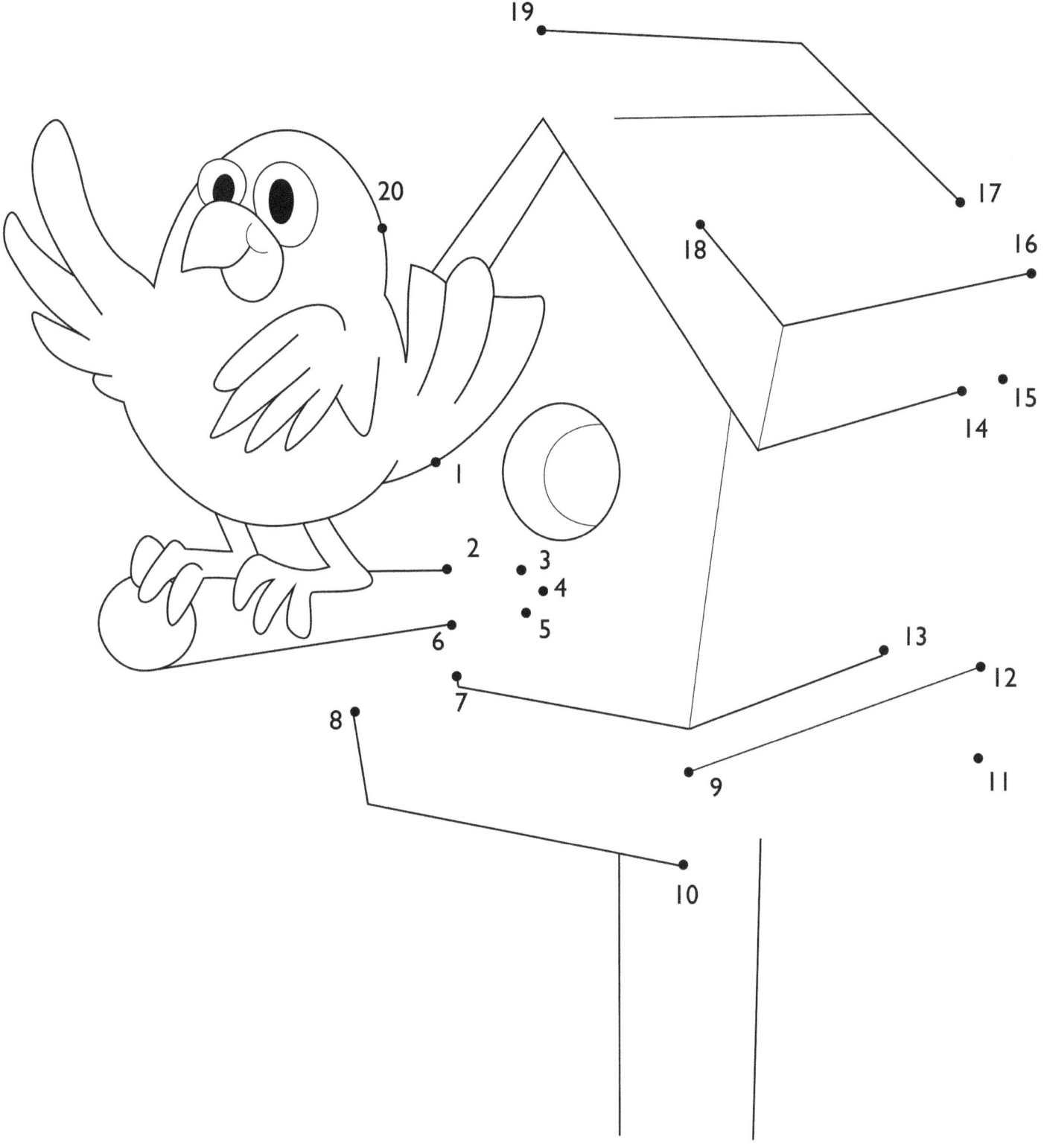

Number review

Count the objects. Color the number to show how many there are.

Name:_____

Number review

Count the objects. Color the number to show how many there are.

135 Denver International SchoolHouse

Number review

Match.

11 eleven

10 ten

8 eight

9 nine

Number review

Sum. Write how many there are.

$$\begin{array}{r}2\\+1\\\hline 3\end{array}$$

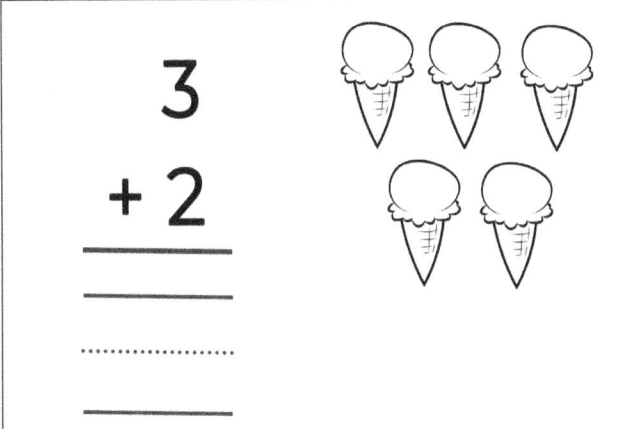

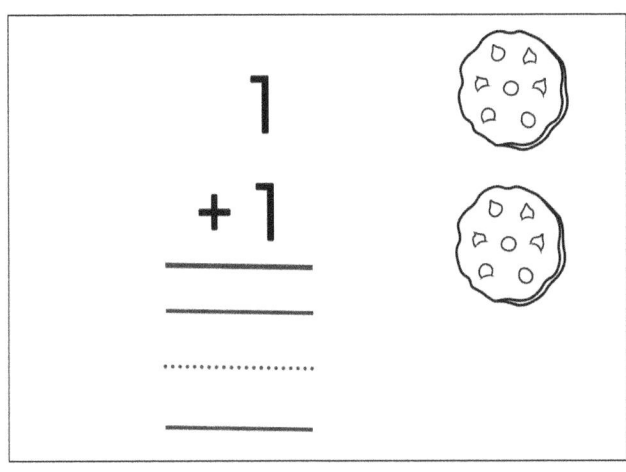

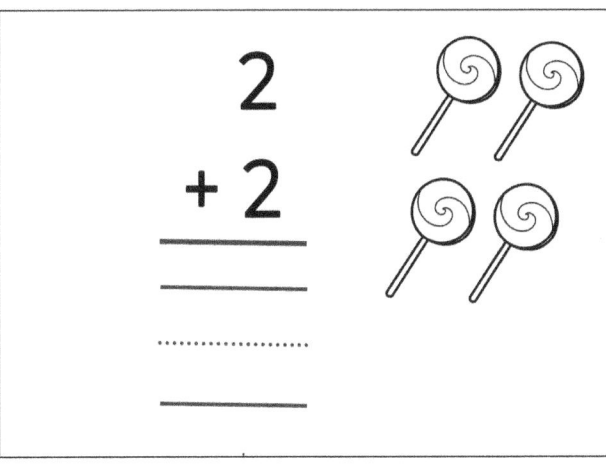

Name:_____

Number review

Match.

   13 thirteen

   12 twelve

   15 fifteen

   14 fourteen

Number review

Sum. Write how many there are.

$$\begin{array}{r}3\\+2\\\hline 5\end{array}$$

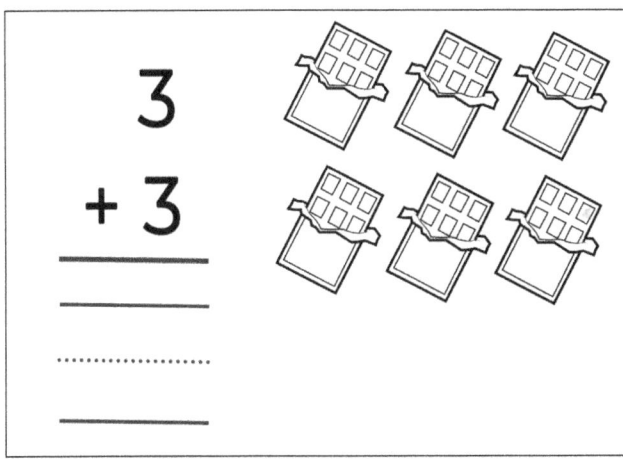

$$\begin{array}{r}3\\+3\\\hline\end{array}$$

$$\begin{array}{r}4\\+3\\\hline\end{array}$$

$$\begin{array}{r}4\\+4\\\hline\end{array}$$

$$\begin{array}{r}5\\+5\\\hline\end{array}$$

$$\begin{array}{r}5\\+4\\\hline\end{array}$$

$$\begin{array}{r}3\\+3\\\hline\end{array}$$

Contact Us:

Web: www.dispreschool.com

Phone: (303) 928-7535

Facebook: @dispreschool

Twitter: @DISPreschool

Address: 6295 S Main St B113, Aurora, CO 80016

www.ingramcontent.com/pod-product-compliance
Lightning Source LLC
Chambersburg PA
CBHW081415080526
44589CB00016B/2543